JUZ 30

عَمَّ

Surah #78
AN-Naba

Makkia

سُورَةُ النَّبَإِ

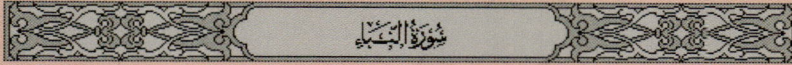

Verses 40
Sections 2

بِسْمِ اللهِ الرَّحْمٰنِ الرَّحِيمِ

				يَتَسَاءَلُونَ	عَمَّ
				yatasaaloona	AAamma
				They are asking one another	About what

﴿ عَمَّ يَتَسَآءَلُونَ ۝ ﴾

1. AAamma yatasaaloona

1 What are they asking (one another)?

			الْعَظِيمِ	ٱلنَّبَإِ	عَنِ
			alAAatheemi	alnnaba-i	AAani
			Great	The news	About

عَنِ ٱلنَّبَإِ ٱلْعَظِيمِ ۝

2. AAani alnnaba-i alAAatheemi

2 About the great news, (i.e. Islamic Monotheism, the Qur'an, which Prophet Muhammad (ﷺ) brought and the Day of Resurrection, etc.),

الَّذِي	هُمْ	فِيهِ	مُخْتَلِفُونَ		

		mukhtalifoona	Feehi	hum	Allathee
		Disagree	In it (about)	They	Which

ٱلَّذِى هُمْ فِيهِ مُخْتَلِفُونَ ﴿٣﴾

3. Allathee hum feehi mukhtalifoona

3 About which they are in disagreement.

			sayaAAlamoona	Kalla
			They will (come to) know	Nay

كَلَّا سَيَعْلَمُونَ ﴿٤﴾

4. Kalla sayaAAlamoona

4 Nay, they will come to know!

			sayaAAlamoona	kalla	Thumma
			They will (come to) know	Nay	Again

ثُمَّ كَلَّا سَيَعْلَمُونَ ﴿٥﴾

5. Thumma kalla sayaAAlamoona

5 Nay, again, they will come to know!

		mihadan	al-arda	najAAli	Alam
		As a bed (vast expanse)	(the) earth	We made	Have not

أَلَمْ نَجْعَلِ ٱلْأَرْضَ مِهَٰدًا ﴿٦﴾

6. Alam najAAli al-arda mihadan

6 Have We not made the earth as a bed,

				awtadan	waaljibala

وَٱلْجِبَالَ أَوْتَادًا

				awtadan	Waaljibala
				(as) pegs	And mountains

وَٱلْجِبَالَ أَوْتَادًا ۝

7. Waaljibala awtadan

7 And the mountains as pegs?

				azwajan	Wakhalaqnakum
				In pairs	And We have created

وَخَلَقْنَٰكُمْ أَزْوَٰجًا ۝

8. Wakhalaqnakum azwajan

8 And We have created you in pairs (male and female, tall and short, good and bad, etc.).

			subatan	nawmakum	WajaAAalna
			For rest	Your sleep	And we have made

وَجَعَلْنَا نَوْمَكُمْ سُبَاتًا ۝

9. WajaAAalna nawmakum subatan

9 And have made your sleep as a thing for rest.

			libasan	allayla	WajaAAalna
			As a covering	The night	And We have made

وَجَعَلْنَا ٱلَّيْلَ لِبَاسًا ۝

10. WajaAAalna allayla libasan

10 And have made the night as a covering (through its darkness),

			maAAashan	alnnahara	WajaAAalna

وَجَعَلْنَا ٱلنَّهَارَ مَعَاشًا

			(for) Livelihood	The day	And We have made

وَجَعَلْنَا ٱلنَّهَارَ مَعَاشًا ۝

11. WajaAAalna alnnahara maAAashan	
11 And have made the day for livelihood.	

		شِدَادًا	سَبْعًا	فَوْقَكُمْ	وَبَنَيْنَا
		shidadan	sabAAan	fawqakum	Wabanayna
		Strong	Seven (Heavens)	Above you	And We have built

وَبَنَيْنَا فَوْقَكُمْ سَبْعًا شِدَادًا ۝

12. Wabanayna fawqakum sabAAan shidadan	
12 And We have built above you seven strong (heavens),	

		وَهَّاجًا	سِرَاجًا	وَجَعَلْنَا
		wahhajan	sirajan	WajaAAalna
		Shinning	Lamp	And We have made

وَجَعَلْنَا سِرَاجًا وَهَّاجًا ۝

13. WajaAAalna sirajan wahhajan	
13 And have made (therein) a shinning lamp (sun).	

	ثَجَّاجًا	مَاءً	ٱلْمُعْصِرَاتِ	مِنَ	وَأَنزَلْنَا
	thajjajan	maan	almuAAsirati	mina	Waanzalna
	Abundant	Water	The rainy clouds	From	And We have sent down

وَأَنزَلْنَا مِنَ ٱلْمُعْصِرَاتِ مَاءً ثَجَّاجًا ۝

14. Waanzalna mina almuAAsirati maan thajjajan	
14 And have sent down from the rainy clouds abundant water.	

	وَنَبَاتًا	حَبًّا	بِهِ	لِنُخْرِجَ
	wanabatan	habban	bihi	Linukhrija
	And vegetation	Corn	Therewith	That We may produce

لِّنُخْرِجَ بِهِۦ حَبًّا وَنَبَاتًا ۝

15. Linukhrija bihi habban wanabatan
15 That We may produce therewith corn and vegetations,

				ٱلْفَافًا	وَجَنَّاتٍ
				alfafan	Wajannatin
				(of) thick growth	And Gardens

وَجَنَّٰتٍ أَلْفَافًا ۝

16. Wajannatin alfafan
16 And gardens of thick growth.

مِيقَٰتًا	كَانَ	ٱلْفَصْلِ	يَوْمَ	إِنَّ
meeqatan	kana	alfasli	yawma	Inna
A fixed time	Is	(of) Decision	(the) day	Verily

إِنَّ يَوْمَ ٱلْفَصْلِ كَانَ مِيقَٰتًا ۝

17. Inna yawma alfasli kana meeqatan
17 Verily, the Day of Decision is a fixed time,

أَفْوَاجًا	فَتَأْتُونَ	ٱلصُّورِ	فِى	يُنفَخُ	يَوْمَ
afwajan	fata/toona	alssoori	fee	yunfakhu	Yawma
In crowds , gates	You shall come forth	The Trumpet	(in)	Will be blown	(The) day (when)

يَوْمَ يُنفَخُ فِى ٱلصُّورِ فَتَأْتُونَ أَفْوَاجًا ۝

18. Yawma yunfakhu fee alssoori fata/toona afwajan
18 The Day when the Trumpet will be blown, and you shall come forth in crowds (groups);

		أَبْوَابًا	فَكَانَتْ	ٱلسَّمَآءُ	وَفُتِحَتِ
		abwaban	fakanat	alssamao	Wafutihati
		(as) doors, gates	It will become	The sky, Heaven	And shall be opened

وَفُتِحَتِ ٱلسَّمَآءُ فَكَانَتْ أَبْوَابًا ۝

19. Wafutihati alssamao fakanat abwaban

And the heaven shall be opened, and it will become as gates,

		سَرَابًا	فَكَانَتْ	الْجِبَالُ	وَسُيِّرَتِ
		saraban	fakanat	aljibalu	Wasuyyirati
		(as) a mirage	They will become	The mountains	And shall be moved away

وَسُيِّرَتِ ٱلْجِبَالُ فَكَانَتْ سَرَابًا ﴿٢٠﴾

20. Wasuyyirati aljibalu fakanat saraban

And the mountains shall be moved away from their places and they will be as if they were a mirage.

		مِرْصَادًا	كَانَ	جَهَنَّمَ	إِنَّ
		mirsadan	kanat	jahannama	Inna
		A place of Ambush	Is	Hell	Truly

إِنَّ جَهَنَّمَ كَانَتْ مِرْصَادًا ﴿٢١﴾

21. Inna jahannama kanat mirsadan

Truly, Hell is a place of ambush,

				مَآبًا	لِّلطَّاغِينَ
				maaban	Lilttagheena
				A dwelling place	For the transgressors

لِّلطَّاغِينَ مَآبًا ﴿٢٢﴾

22. Lilttagheena maaban

A dwelling place for the *Taghun* (those who transgress the boundry limits set by Allah like polytheists, disbelievers in the Oneness of Allah, hyprocrites, sinners, criminals, etc.),

			أَحْقَابًا	فِيهَا	لَابِثِينَ
			ahqaban	feeha	Labitheena
			For ages	Therein	They will dwell (abide)

لَّابِثِينَ فِيهَا أَحْقَابًا ﴿٢٣﴾

23. Labitheena feeha ahqaban

They will abide therein for ages,

شَرَابًا	وَلَا	بَرْدًا	فِيهَا	يَذُوقُونَ	لَّا
sharaban	wala	bardan	feeha	yathooqoona	La
(any) drink	Nor	Cool	Therein	They will taste	Not

لَّا يَذُوقُونَ فِيهَا بَرْدًا وَلَا شَرَابًا ﴿٢٤﴾

24. La yathooqoona feeha bardan wala sharaban
Nothing cool shall they taste therein, nor any drink.

			وَغَسَّاقًا	حَمِيمًا	إِلَّا
			Waghassaqan	hameeman	Illa
			And (dirty wound discharges) Pus	Boiling water	Except

إِلَّا حَمِيمًا وَغَسَّاقًا ﴿٢٥﴾

25. Illa hameeman waghassaqan
Except boiling water, and dirty wound discharges.

				وِفَاقًا	جَزَاءً
				wifaqan	Jazaan
				Fitting	As a recompense

جَزَاءً وِفَاقًا ﴿٢٦﴾

26. Jazaan wifaqan
An exact recompense (according to their evil crimes).

حِسَابًا	يَرْجُونَ	لَا	كَانُوا	إِنَّهُمْ
hisaban	yarjoona	la	kanoo	Innahum
A reckoning Account	Expecting looking for	Not	Were	Verily they

إِنَّهُمْ كَانُوا لَا يَرْجُونَ حِسَابًا ﴿٢٧﴾

27. Innahum kanoo la yarjoona hisaban
For verily, they used not to look for a reckoning.

			كِذَّابًا	بِآيَاتِنَا	وَكَذَّبُوا
			kiththaban	bi-ayatina	Wakaththaboo
			In complete rejection	Our signs	And they denied

وَكَذَّبُوا بِآيَاتِنَا كِذَّابًا ﴿٢٨﴾

28. Wakaththaboo bi-ayatina kiththaban
But they belied Our *Ayat* (proofs, evidences, verses, lessons, signs, revelations, and that which Our Prophet (Peace be upon him) brought) completely.

		كِتَابًا	أَحْصَيْنَاهُ	شَيْءٍ	وَكُلَّ
		kitaban	Ahsaynahu	shay-in	Wakulla
		(in) a book	We have recorded	Thing	And every

وَكُلَّ شَيْءٍ أَحْصَيْنَاهُ كِتَابًا ﴿٢٩﴾

29. Wakulla shay-in ahsaynahu kitaban
And all things We have recorded in a Book.

عَذَابًا	إِلَّا	نَّزِيدَكُمْ	فَلَن	فَذُوقُوا
AAathaban	illa	nazeedakum	falan	Fathooqoo
(in) torment	Except	We sall give you increase	So not	So you taste

فَذُوقُوا فَلَن نَّزِيدَكُمْ إِلَّا عَذَابًا ﴿٣٠﴾

30. Fathooqoo falan nazeedakum illa AAathaban
So taste you (the results of your evil actions); no increase shall We give you, except in torment.

Section 2

		مَفَازًا	لِلْمُتَّقِينَ	إِنَّ
		mafazan	lilmuttaqeena	Inna
		(will be) a success	For the righteous	Verily

إِنَّ لِلْمُتَّقِينَ مَفَازًا ﴿٣١﴾

31. Inna lilmuttaqeena mafazan

Verily, for the *Muttaqun*, there will be a success (Paradise);

				وَأَعْنَابًا	حَدَائِقَ
				waaAAnaban	Hada-iqa
				And grapes	Gardens

حَدَآئِقَ وَأَعْنَـٰبًا ﴿٣٢﴾

32. Hada-iqa waaAAnaban
Gardens and grapeyards;

				أَتْرَابًا	وَكَوَاعِبَ
				atraban	WakawaAAiba
				Of equal age	And buxon girls

وَكَوَاعِبَ أَتْرَابًا ﴿٣٣﴾

33. WakawaAAiba atraban
And young full-breasted (mature) maidens of equal age;

				دِهَاقًا	وَكَأْسًا
				dihaqan	Waka/san
				Filled/full	And cup

وَكَأْسًا دِهَاقًا ﴿٣٤﴾

34. Waka/san dihaqan
And a full cup (of wine).

كِذَّابًا	وَلَا	لَغْوًا	فِيهَا	يَسْمَعُونَ	لَّا
kiththaban	wala	laghwan	feeha	yasmaAAoona	La
Lying	Nor	Vain talk	therein	They shall hear	Not

لَّا يَسْمَعُونَ فِيهَا لَغْوًا وَلَا كِذَّابًا ﴿٣٥﴾

35. La yasmaAAoona feeha laghwan wala kiththaban
No *Laghw* (dirty, false, evil talk) shall they hear therein, nor lying;

جَزَاء	مِّن	رَّبِّكَ	عَطَاء	حِسَابًا
Jazaan	min	rabbika	AAataan	hisaban
A reward, recompense	From	Your Lord	A gift	An example calculated

جَزَآءً مِّن رَّبِّكَ عَطَآءً حِسَابًا ﴿٣٦﴾

36. Jazaan min rabbika AAataan hisaban

A reward from your Lord, an ample calculated gift (according to the best of their good deeds).

رَبِّ	السَّمَاوَاتِ	وَالْأَرْضِ	وَمَا	بَيْنَهُمَا	الرَّحْمَنِ
Rabbi	alssamawati	waal-ardi	wama	baynahuma	alrrahmani
Lord	(of the) Heavens	And the earth	And whatever	(is) between them	The Most Gracious

لَا	يَمْلِكُونَ	مِنْهُ	خِطَابًا		
la	yamlikoona	minhu	khitaban		
Not	They have power	With Him	To speak		

رَّبِّ ٱلسَّمَـٰوَٰتِ وَٱلْأَرْضِ وَمَا بَيْنَهُمَا ٱلرَّحْمَـٰنِ ۖ لَا يَمْلِكُونَ مِنْهُ خِطَابًا ﴿٣٧﴾

37. Rabbi alssamawati waal-ardi wama baynahuma alrrahmani la yamlikoona minhu khitaban

(From) the Lord of the heavens and the earth, and whatsoever is in between them, the Most Beneficent, none can dare to speak with Him (on the Day of Resurrection except after His Leave).

يَوْمَ	يَقُومُ	الرُّوحُ	وَالْمَلَائِكَةُ	صَفًّا	لَّا
Yawma	yaqoomu	alroohu	waalmala-ikatu	saffan	la
(the) Day (when)	Will stand	The spirit (Gabriel)	And the angels	In rows	Not

يَتَكَلَّمُون	إِلَّا	مَنْ	أَذِنَ	لَهُ	الرَّحْمَنُ
yatakallamoona	illa	man	athina	lahu	alrrahmanu
They will speak	Except	Him	Gives permission, allows	(for him) whom	The most gracious

	صَوَابًا	وَقَالَ
	sawaban	waqala
	Right	And He will say, speak

يَوْمَ يَقُومُ ٱلرُّوحُ وَٱلْمَلَـٰئِكَةُ صَفًّا ۖ لَّا يَتَكَلَّمُونَ إِلَّا مَنْ أَذِنَ لَهُ ٱلرَّحْمَـٰنُ وَقَالَ صَوَابًا ﴿٣٨﴾

38. Yawma yaqoomu alrroohu waalmala-ikatu saffan la yatakallamoona illa man athina lahu alrrahmanu waqala sawaban

The Day that *Ar-Ruh* [Jibrael (Gabriel) or another angel] and the angels will stand forth in rows, none shall speak except him whom the Most Beneficent (Allah) allows, and he will speak what is right.

ٱتَّخَذَ	شَاءَ	فَمَن	ٱلْحَقُّ	ٱلْيَوْمُ	ذَٰلِكَ
ittakhatha	shaa	faman	alhaqqu	alyawmu	Thalika
He will take	Wishes , wills	So whosoever	The true	The day	That (is)

			مَآبًا	رَّبِّهِ	إِلَىٰ
			maaban	rabbihi	ila
			A place	His Lord	Towards / with

ذَٰلِكَ ٱلْيَوْمُ ٱلْحَقُّ ۖ فَمَن شَاءَ ٱتَّخَذَ إِلَىٰ رَبِّهِ مَآبًا ﴿٣٩﴾

39. Thalika alyawmu alhaqqu faman shaa ittakhatha ila rabbihi maaban

That is without doubt the True Day, so, whosoever wills, let him seek a place with (or a way to) His Lord (by obeying Him in this worldly life)!

يَنظُرُ	يَوْمَ	قَرِيبًا	عَذَابًا	أَنذَرْنَاكُمْ	إِنَّا
yanthuru	yawma	qareeban	AAathaban	antharnakum	Inna
Will see	The Day (when)	Near	(od) a torment	Have wrned you	Verily We

ٱلْكَافِرُ	يَقُولُ	يَدَاهُ	قَدَّمَتْ	مَا	ٱلْمَرْءُ
alkafiru	wayaqoolu	yadahu	qaddamat	ma	almaro
The disbelievers	And will say	His hands	Have sent forth	Whicn	Man

			تُرَابًا	كُنتُ	لَيْتَنِي	يَا
			turaban	kuntu	laytanee	ya
			Dust	I were	Would that	Woe to me

إِنَّا أَنذَرْنَٰكُمْ عَذَابًا قَرِيبًا يَوْمَ يَنظُرُ ٱلْمَرْءُ مَا قَدَّمَتْ يَدَاهُ وَيَقُولُ ٱلْكَافِرُ يَٰلَيْتَنِى كُنتُ تُرَٰبًۢا ۞

40. Inna antharnakum AAathaban qareeban yawma yanthuru almaro ma qaddamat yadahu wayaqoolu alkafiru ya laytanee kuntu turaban

Verily, We have warned you of a near torment, the Day when man will see that (the deeds) which his hands have sent forth, and the disbeliever will say: "Woe to me! Would that I were dust!"

Surah # 79
AN-NAZIAT

Makkia

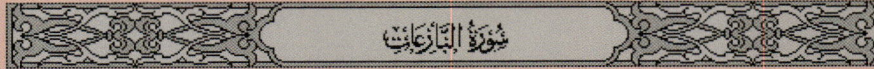

Verses 46
Sections 2

بِسْمِ ٱللَّهِ ٱلرَّحْمَٰنِ ٱلرَّحِيمِ

				غَرْقًا	وَٱلنَّازِعَاتِ
				gharqan	WaalnnaziAAati
				With violence	By those (angels) who tear you out (the souls of the disbelievers)

﴿ وَٱلنَّٰزِعَٰتِ غَرْقًا ﴾ ۝

1. WaalnnaziAAati gharqan

By those (angels) who pull out (the souls of the disbelievers and the wicked) with great violence;

				نَشْطًا	وَٱلنَّاشِطَاتِ
				nashtan	Waalnnashitati
				Gently	By those

					(angels) who draw out (the souls of the believers

وَٱلنَّـٰشِطَـٰتِ نَشْطًا ۝

2. Waalnnashitati nashtan

By those (angels) who gently take out (the souls of the believers);

				سَبْحًا	وَٱلسَّـٰبِحَاتِ
				sabhan	Waalssabihati
				Swifly	By those who swim

وَٱلسَّـٰبِحَـٰتِ سَبْحًا ۝

3. Waalssabihati sabhan

And by those that swim along (i.e. angels or planets in their orbits, etc.).

				سَبْقًا	فَٱلسَّـٰبِقَاتِ
				sabqan	Faalssabiqati
				In a race	And by those (angels) who press forward

فَٱلسَّـٰبِقَـٰتِ سَبْقًا ۝

4. Faalssabiqati sabqan

And by those that press forward as in a race (i.e. the angels or stars or the horses, etc.).

				أَمْرًا	فَٱلْمُدَبِّرَاتِ
				Amran	Faalmudabbirati
				The commands (of their Lord)	And by those (angels) who arrange to execute

فَٱلْمُدَبِّرَٰتِ أَمْرًا ۝

5. Faalmudabbirati amran

And by those angels who arrange to do the Commands of their Lord, (so verily, you disbelievers will be called to account).

			الرَّاجِفَةُ	تَرْجُفُ	يَوْمَ
			alrrajifatu	tarjufu	Yawma
			The trembling / the first blowing of he Trumpet	Shakes	(on) the day

يَوْمَ تَرْجُفُ ٱلرَّاجِفَةُ ﴿٦﴾

6. Yawma tarjufu alrrajifatu

On the Day (when the first blowing of the Trumpet is blown), the earth and the mountains will shake violently (and everybody will die),

			الرَّادِفَةُ	تَتْبَعُهَا
			alrradifatu	TatbaAAuha
			That which is subsequent (the second blowing of the Trumpet	Follows i

تَتْبَعُهَا ٱلرَّادِفَةُ ﴿٧﴾

7. TatbaAAuha alrradifatu

The second blowing of the Trumpet follows it (and everybody will be raised up),

			وَاجِفَةٌ	يَوْمَئِذٍ	قُلُوبٌ
			wajifatun	yawma-ithin	Quloobun
			Will beat (with fear)	That day	Hearts

قُلُوبٌ يَوْمَئِذٍ وَاجِفَةٌ ﴿٨﴾

8. Quloobun yawma-ithin wajifatun

(Some) hearts that Day will shake with fear and anxiety.

			خَاشِعَةٌ	أَبْصَارُهَا
			khashiAAatun	Absaruha
			(will be) downcast	Their eyes

أَبْصَـٰرُهَا خَـٰشِعَةٌ ۝

9. Absaruha khashiAAatun

Their eyes cast down.

الْحَافِرَةِ	فِي	لَمَرْدُودُونَ	أَئِنَّا	يَقُولُونَ
alhafirati	fee	lamardoodoona	a-inna	Yaqooloona
The former state of life	To (in)	Be returned	Shall we indeed	They say

يَقُولُونَ أَئِنَّا لَمَرْدُودُونَ فِي ٱلْحَافِرَةِ ۝

10. Yaqooloona a-inna lamardoodoona fee alhafirati

They say: "Shall we indeed be returned to (our) former state of life?

نَّخِرَةً	عِظَامًا	كُنَّا	أَئِذَا
nakhiratan	AAithaman	kunna	A-itha
Crumbled	Bones	We are	Even after

أَءِذَا كُنَّا عِظَـٰمًا نَّخِرَةً ۝

11. A-itha kunna AAithaman nakhiratan

"Even after we are crumbled bones?"

خَاسِرَةٌ	كَرَّةٌ	إِذًا	تِلْكَ	قَالُوا
khasiratun	karratun	ithan	tilka	Qaloo
With loss	(would be) a return	In that case	That	They say

قَالُوا تِلْكَ إِذًا كَرَّةٌ خَاسِرَةٌ ۝

12. Qaloo tilka ithan karratun khasiratun

They say: "It would in that case, be a return with loss!"

وَاحِدَةٌ	زَجْرَةٌ	هِيَ	فَإِنَّمَا
wahidatun	zajratun	hiya	Fa-innama
A single	Cry	It (will be)	But only

15

$$\text{فَإِنَّمَا هِيَ زَجْرَةٌ وَّاحِدَةٌ ۝}$$

13. Fa-innama hiya zajratun wahidatun

But only, it will be a single *Zajrah* [shout (i.e., the second blowing of the Trumpet)]. (See Verse 37:19).

		بِالسَّاهِرَةِ	هُم	فَإِذَا
		bialssahirati	hum	Fa-itha
		(will be) awakened (alive after death)	They	When (behold)

$$\text{فَإِذَا هُم بِالسَّاهِرَةِ ۝}$$

14. Fa-itha hum bialssahirati

When, behold, they find themselves over the earth alive after their death,

	مُوسَى	حَدِيثُ	أَتَاكَ	هَلْ
	moosa	hadeethu	ataka	Hal
	(of) Musa (Moses)	Story	Come to you	Has there

$$\text{هَلْ أَتَاكَ حَدِيثُ مُوسَى ۝}$$

15. Hal ataka hadeethu moosa

Has there come to you the story of Musa (Moses)?

طُوًى	الْمُقَدَّسِ	بِالْوَادِ	رَبُّهُ	نَادَاهُ	إِذْ
tuwan	almuqaddasi	bialwadi	rabbuhu	nadahu	Ith
Of Tuwa	Sacred	In the valley	His Lord	Called him	When

$$\text{إِذْ نَادَاهُ رَبُّهُ بِالْوَادِ الْمُقَدَّسِ طُوًى ۝}$$

16. Ith nadahu rabbuhu bialwadi almuqaddasi tuwan

When his Lord called him in the sacred valley of Tuwa,

طَغَى	إِنَّهُ	فِرْعَوْنَ	إِلَى	اذْهَبْ
tagha	innahu	firAAawna	ila	Ithhab
Has transgressed all bounds	verily he	Pharaoh	To	You go

آذْهَبْ إِلَىٰ فِرْعَوْنَ إِنَّهُ طَغَىٰ ۝

17. Ithhab ila firAAawna innahu tagha

Go to Fir'aun (Pharaoh), verily, he has transgressed all bounds (in crimes, sins, polytheism, disbelief, etc.).

تَزَكَّىٰ	أَن	إِلَىٰ	لَّكَ	هَل	فَقُلْ
tazakka	an	ila	laka	hal	Faqul
You purify yourself	until		For you	Is it	And say

فَقُلْ هَل لَّكَ إِلَىٰ أَن تَزَكَّىٰ ۝

18. Faqul hal laka ila an tazakka

And say to him: "Would you purify yourself (from the sin of disbelief by becoming a believer)",

		فَتَخْشَىٰ	رَبِّكَ	إِلَىٰ	وَأَهْدِيَكَ
		fatakhsha	rabbika	ila	Waahdiyaka
		So you should fear (Him)	Your Lord	To	And I guide you

وَأَهْدِيَكَ إِلَىٰ رَبِّكَ فَتَخْشَىٰ ۝

19. Waahdiyaka ila rabbika fatakhsha

And that I guide you to your Lord, so you should fear Him?

			الْكُبْرَىٰ	الْآيَةَ	فَأَرَاهُ
			alkubra	al-ayata	Faarahu
			Great	The sign	Then He showed him

فَأَرَاهُ الْآيَةَ الْكُبْرَىٰ ۝

20. Faarahu al-ayata alkubra

Then [Musa (Moses)] showed him the great sign (miracles).

				وَعَصَىٰ	فَكَذَّبَ
				waAAasa	Fakaththaba
				And Disobeyed	But He denied

17

فَكَذَّبَ وَعَصَىٰ ﴿٢١﴾

21. Fakaththaba waAAasa

But [Fir'aun (Pharaoh)] belied and disobeyed;

			يَسْعَىٰ	أَدْبَرَ	ثُمَّ
			yasAAa	adbara	Thumma
			Striving (against Allah)	He turned his back	Then

ثُمَّ أَدْبَرَ يَسْعَىٰ ﴿٢٢﴾

22. Thumma adbara yasAAa

Then he turned his back, striving hard (against Allah).

				فَنَادَىٰ	فَحَشَرَ
				fanada	Fahashara
				And cried Loud	Then He gathered (his people)

فَحَشَرَ فَنَادَىٰ ﴿٢٣﴾

23. Fahashara fanada

Then he gathered his people and cried aloud,

	الْأَعْلَىٰ	رَبُّكُمُ	أَنَا	فَقَالَ
	al-aAAla	rabbukumu	ana	Faqala
	Most high	(am) yor Lord	I	And said

فَقَالَ أَنَا رَبُّكُمُ الْأَعْلَىٰ ﴿٢٤﴾

24. Faqala ana rabbukumu al-aAAla

Saying: "I am your lord, most high",

وَالْأُولَىٰ	الْآخِرَةِ	نَكَالَ	اللَّهُ	فَأَخَذَهُ
waal-oola	al-akhirati	nakala	Allahu	Faakhathahu
And the first	For the last	(with) punishment	Allah	So seized him

18

فَأَخَذَهُ ٱللَّهُ نَكَالَ ٱلْأَخِرَةِ وَٱلْأُولَىٰ ﴿٢٥﴾

25. Faakhathahu Allahu nakala al-akhirati waal-oola

So Allah, seized him with punishment for his last [i.e. his saying: "I am your lord, most high") (see Verse 79:24)] and first [(i.e. his saying, "O chiefs! I know not that you have a god other than I" (see Verse 28:38)] transgression.

يَخْشَىٰ	لِّمَن	لَعِبْرَةً	ذَٰلِكَ	فِي	إِنَّ
yakhsha	liman	laAAibratan	thalika	fee	Inna
Fears (Allah)	For whosoever	(is) an admonition	This	In	Verily

إِنَّ فِي ذَٰلِكَ لَعِبْرَةً لِّمَن تَخْشَىٰ ﴿٢٦﴾

26. Inna fee thalika laAAibratan liman yakhsha

Verily, in this is an instructive admonition for whosoever fears Allah.

Section 2

بَنَاهَا	السَّمَاءُ	أَمِ	خَلْقًا	أَشَدُّ	أَأَنتُمْ
banaha	alssamao	ami	khalqan	ashaddu	Aantum
That He constructed	The Heaven	Or	To create	More difficult	Are you

أَءَأَنتُمْ أَشَدُّ خَلْقًا أَمِ ٱلسَّمَآءُ بَنَىٰهَا ﴿٢٧﴾

27. Aantum ashaddu khalqan ami alssamao banaha

Are you more difficult to create, or is the heaven that He constructed?

			فَسَوَّاهَا	سَمْكَهَا	رَفَعَ
			fasawwaha	samkaha	RafaAAa
			And He has equally ordered it (perfectly)	Its heights	He raised

رَفَعَ سَمْكَهَا فَسَوَّىٰهَا ﴿٢٨﴾

28. RafaAAa samkaha fasawwaha

He raised its height, and He has equally ordered it,

		دُحَاهَا	وَأَخْرَجَ	لَيْلَهَا	وَأَغْطَشَ
		duhaha	waakhraja	laylaha	Waaghtasha
		Its forenoon	And He brings	Its night	And He covers

			out	with darkness

وَأَغْطَشَ لَيْلَهَا وَأَخْرَجَ ضُحَىٰهَا ﴿٢٩﴾

29. Waaghtasha laylaha waakhraja duhaha
Its night He covers with darkness, and its forenoon He brings out (with light).

دَحَاهَا	ذَٰلِكَ	بَعْدَ	وَالْأَرْضَ
dahaha	thalika	baAAda	Waal-arda
He spreads it	That	After	And the Earth

وَالْأَرْضَ بَعْدَ ذَٰلِكَ دَحَاهَا ﴿٣٠﴾

30. Waal-arda baAAda thalika dahaha
And after that He spreads the earth;

وَمَرْعَاهَا	مَاءَهَا	مِنْهَا	أَخْرَجَ
wamarAAaha	maaha	minha	Akhraja
And its pasture	Its water	Therefrom	And He brought forth

أَخْرَجَ مِنْهَا مَاءَهَا وَمَرْعَاهَا ﴿٣١﴾

31. Akhraja minha maaha wamarAAaha
And brought forth therefrom its water and its pasture;

			أَرْسَاهَا	وَالْجِبَالَ
			arsaha	Waaljibala
			He has fixed them firmly	And the mountains

وَالْجِبَالَ أَرْسَاهَا ﴿٣٢﴾

32. Waaljibala arsaha
And the mountains He has fixed firmly;

			وَلِأَنْعَامِكُمْ	لَّكُمْ	مَتَاعًا
			wali-anAAamikum	lakum	MataAAan
			And your cattle	For You	To be a provision and

				benefit

مَتَـٰعًا لَّكُمْ وَلِأَنْعَـٰمِكُمْ ۝

33. MataAAan lakum wali-anAAamikum
(To be) a provision and benefit for you and your cattle.

		الْكُبْرَى	الطَّامَّةُ	جَاءَتِ	فَإِذَا
		alkubra	alttammatu	jaati	Fa-itha
		The greatest	The catastrophe	Comes	But when

فَإِذَا جَاءَتِ الطَّآمَّةُ الْكُبْرَىٰ ۝

34. Fa-itha jaati alttammatu alkubra
But when there comes the greatest catastrophe (i.e. the Day of Recompense, etc.),

سَعَى	مَا	الْإِنْسَانُ	يَتَذَكَّرُ	يَوْمَ
saAAa	ma	al-insanu	yatathakkaru	Yawma
Has strove for	What	Man	Shall remember	Day (when)

يَوْمَ يَتَذَكَّرُ ٱلْإِنسَـٰنُ مَا سَعَىٰ ۝

35. Yawma yatathakkaru al-insanu ma saAAa
The Day when man shall remember what he strove for,

	يَرَى	لِمَن	الْجَحِيمُ	وَبُرِّزَتِ
	yara	liman	aljaheemu	Waburrizati
	Sees	For one who	Hell-fire	And shall be made apparent in full view

وَبُرِّزَتِ ٱلْجَحِيمُ لِمَن يَرَىٰ ۝

36. Waburrizati aljaheemu liman yara
And Hell-fire shall be made apparent in full view for (every) one who sees,

			طَغَى	مَن	فَأَمَّا
			tagha	man	Faamma
			Has transgressed	Him who	Then for

			all bounds		

فَأَمَّا مَن طَغَىٰ ۝

37. Faamma man tagha
Then, for him who *Tagha* (transgressed all bounds, in disbelief, oppression and evil deeds of disobedience to Allah).

			الدُّنْيَا	الْحَيَاةَ	وَآثَرَ
			alddunya	alhayata	Waathara
			worldly	The life	And preffered

وَءَاثَرَ ٱلْحَيَوٰةَ ٱلدُّنْيَا ۝

38. Waathara alhayata alddunya
And preferred the life of this world (by following his evil desires and lusts),

		الْمَأْوَىٰ	هِيَ	الْجَحِيمَ	فَإِنَّ
		alma/wa	hiya	Aljaheema	Fa-inna
		(wll be his) abode	(it)	Hell-fire	Then verily

فَإِنَّ ٱلْجَحِيمَ هِيَ ٱلْمَأْوَىٰ ۝

39. Fa-inna aljaheema hiya alma/wa
Verily, his abode will be Hell-fire;

وَنَهَى	رَبِّهِ	مَقَامَ	خَافَ	مَنْ	وَأَمَّا
wanaha	Rabbihi	maqama	khafa	man	Waama
And restrained	His Lord	Standing (before)	Who feared	Him	But as for

		الْهَوَى	عَنِ	النَّفْسَ	
		alhawa	AAani	alnnafsa	
		Evil/desires/ Lust	From	Himself	

وَأَمَّا مَنْ خَافَ مَقَامَ رَبِّهِۦ وَنَهَى ٱلنَّفْسَ عَنِ ٱلْهَوَىٰ ۝

40. Waama man khafa maqama rabbihi wanaha alnnafsa AAani alhawa
But as for him who feared standing before his Lord, and restrained himself from impure evil desires, and lusts.

		الْمَأْوَى	هِيَ	الْجَنَّةَ	فَإِنَّ
		alma/wa	hiya	aljannata	Fa-inna
		(will be his) abode	(it)	Paradise	Then verily

فَإِنَّ ٱلْجَنَّةَ هِيَ ٱلْمَأْوَىٰ ﴿٤١﴾

41. Fa-inna aljannata hiya alma/wa

مُرْسَاهَا	أَيَّانَ	السَّاعَةِ	عَنِ	يَسْأَلُونَكَ
mursaha	ayyana	alssaAAati	AAani	Yas-aloonaka
(will be) its appointed time	When	The Hour	About	They ask you

يَسْـَٔلُونَكَ عَنِ ٱلسَّاعَةِ أَيَّانَ مُرْسَىٰهَا ﴿٤٢﴾

42. Yas-aloonaka AAani alssaAAati ayyana mursaha

They ask you (O Muhammad (ﷺ)) about the Hour, - when will be its appointed time?

	ذِكْرَاهَا	مِن	أَنتَ	فِيمَ
	thikraha	min	anta	Feema
	(its) knowledge	Any	You have	About which not

فِيمَ أَنتَ مِن ذِكْرَىٰهَآ ﴿٤٣﴾

43. Feema anta min thikraha

You have no knowledge to say anything about it,

		مُنتَهَاهَا	رَبِّكَ	إِلَى
		muntahaha	rabbika	Ila
		(belongs) the term thereof	Your Land	To

إِلَىٰ رَبِّكَ مُنتَهَىٰهَآ ﴿٤٤﴾

44. Ila rabbika muntahaha

To your Lord belongs (the knowledge of) the term thereof?

إِنَّمَا	أَنتَ	مُنذِرٌ	مَن	يَخْشَاهَا
Innama	anta	munthiru	man	yakhshaha
Only	You	(are) a warner	(for) those who	Fear it

إِنَّمَآ أَنتَ مُنذِرُ مَن تَخْشَاهَا ﴿٤٥﴾

45. Innama anta munthiru man yakhshaha

You (O Muhammad ﷺ) are only a warner for those who fear it,

كَأَنَّهُمْ	يَوْمَ	يَرَوْنَهَا	لَمْ	يَلْبَثُوا	إِلَّا
Kaannahum	yawma	yarawnaha	lam	yalbathoo	illa
As if they	The day	They see it	Not	They are tarried	Except

عَشِيَّةً	أَوْ	ضُحَاهَا			
AAashiyyatan	aw	duhaha			
An afternoon	Or	Its morning			

كَأَنَّهُمْ يَوْمَ يَرَوْنَهَا لَمْ يَلْبَثُوٓا۟ إِلَّا عَشِيَّةً أَوْ ضُحَٰهَا ﴿٤٦﴾

46. Kaannahum yawma yarawnaha lam yalbathoo illa AAashiyyatan aw duhaha

The Day they see it, (it will be) as if they had not tarried (in this world) except an afternoon or a morning.

Surah # 80
ABASA

Makkia

سورة عبس

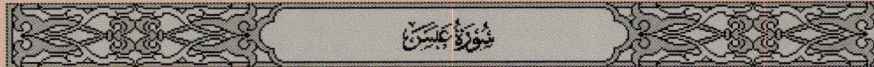

Verses 42
Section 1

بِسْمِ اللَّهِ الرَّحْمَٰنِ الرَّحِيمِ

عَبَسَ	وَتَوَلَّى			
AAabasa	watawalla			
He frowned	And turned away			

بِسْمِ عَبَسَ وَتَوَلَّىٰ ۝

1. AAabasa watawalla

(The Prophet (ﷺ)) frowned and turned away,

			الْأَعْمَىٰ	جَاءَهُ	أَن
			al-aAAma	jaahu	An
			The Blind man	came to him	Because

أَن جَاءَهُ الْأَعْمَىٰ ۝

2. An jaahu al-aAAma

Because there came to him the blind man (i.e. 'Abdullah bin Umm-Maktum, who came to the Prophet (ﷺ) while he was preaching to one or some of the Quraish chiefs).

		يَزَّكَّىٰ	لَعَلَّهُ	يُدْرِيكَ	وَمَا
		yazzakka	laAAallahu	yudreeka	Wama
		Might become pure	That He	(could) inform you	And what

وَمَا يُدْرِيكَ لَعَلَّهُ يَزَّكَّىٰ ۝

3. Wama yudreeka laAAallahu yazzakka

But what could tell you that per chance he might become pure (from sins)?

		الذِّكْرَىٰ	فَتَنفَعَهُ	يَذَّكَّرُ	أَوْ
		alththikra	fatanfaAAahu	yaththakkaru	Aw
		The admonition	And might profit him	Might receive admonition	Or

أَوْ يَذَّكَّرُ فَتَنفَعَهُ الذِّكْرَىٰ ۝

4. Aw yaththakkaru fatanfaAAahu alththikra

Or that he might receive admonition, and that the admonition might profit him?

			اسْتَغْنَىٰ	مَنِ	أَمَّا
			istaghna	mani	Amma
			Thinks himself self-sufficient	Him who	As for

أَمَّا مَنِ ٱسْتَغْنَىٰ ﴿٥﴾

5. Amma mani istaghna
As for him who thinks himself self-sufficient,

			تَصَدَّىٰ	لَهُۥ	فَأَنتَ
			Tasadda	lahu	Faanta
			Attend	To him	So you

فَأَنتَ لَهُۥ تَصَدَّىٰ ﴿٦﴾

6. Faanta lahu tasadda
To him you attend;

	يَزَّكَّىٰ	أَلَّا	عَلَيْكَ	وَمَا
	yazzakka	alla	AAalayka	Wama
	He will become pure	If not	(is) upon yo	And what

وَمَا عَلَيْكَ أَلَّا يَزَّكَّىٰ ﴿٧﴾

7. Wama AAalayka alla yazzakka
What does it matter to you if he will not become pure (from disbelief, you are only a Messenger, your duty is to convey the Message of Allah).

	يَسْعَىٰ	جَاءَكَ	مَن	وَأَمَّا
	yasAAa	jaaka	man	Waamma
	Running	Came to you	Him who	But as to

وَأَمَّا مَن جَاءَكَ يَسْعَىٰ ﴿٨﴾

8. Waamma man jaaka yasAAa
But as to him who came to you running.

			يَخْشَىٰ	وَهُوَ
			yakhsha	Wahuwa
			Is afraid	And He

وَهُوَ يَخْشَىٰ ﴿٩﴾

26

9. Wahuwa yakhsha
And is afraid (of Allah and His Punishment),

			تَلَهَّىٰ	عَنْهُ	فَأَنتَ
			talahha	AAanhu	Faanta
			Are unmindful , neglectful	From him	So you

$$\text{فَأَنتَ عَنْهُ تَلَهَّىٰ ﴿١٠﴾}$$

10. Faanta AAanhu talahha
Of him you are neglectful and divert your attention to another,

			تَذْكِرَةٌ	إِنَّهَا	كَلَّا
			tathkiratun	innaha	Kalla
			An admonition	Indeed it is	Nay

$$\text{كَلَّا إِنَّهَا تَذْكِرَةٌ ﴿١١﴾}$$

11. Kalla innaha tathkiratun
Nay, (do not do like this), indeed it (these Verses of this Qur'an) are an admonition,

			ذَكَرَهُ	شَاءَ	فَمَن
			Thakarahu	shaa	Faman
			He should remember it	Wills	So whosoever

$$\text{فَمَن شَاءَ ذَكَرَهُ ﴿١٢﴾}$$

12. Faman shaa thakarahu
So whoever wills, let him pay attention to it.

			مُكَرَّمَةٍ	صُحُفٍ	فِي
			mukarramatin	suhufin	Fee
			Honoured	Scriptures, Records	In

$$\text{فِي صُحُفٍ مُّكَرَّمَةٍ ﴿١٣﴾}$$

13. Fee suhufin mukarramatin
(It is) in Records held (greatly) in honour (*Al-Lauh Al-Mahfuz*).

				مُّطَهَّرَةٍ	مَّرْفُوعَةٍ
				muṭahharatin	MarfooAAatin
				Purified	Exalted

مَّرْفُوعَةٍ مُّطَهَّرَةٍ ﴿١٤﴾

14. MarfooAAatin muṭahharatin
Exalted (in dignity), purified,

				سَفَرَةٍ	بِأَيْدِي
				Safaratin	Bi-aydee
				(of) scribes (angels)	In the Hands

بِأَيْدِى سَفَرَةٍ ﴿١٥﴾

15. Bi-aydee safaratin
In the hands of scribes (angels).

				بَرَرَةٍ	كِرَامٍ
				Bararatin	Kiramin
				Obiedient, pious	Honourable

كِرَامٍ بَرَرَةٍ ﴿١٦﴾

16. Kiramin bararatin
Honourable and obedient.

		أَكْفَرَهُ	مَا	الْإِنسَانُ	قُتِلَ
		akfarahu	ma	al-insanu	Qutila
		ungrateful he is	How	The man	(be cursed) be killed

قُتِلَ ٱلْإِنسَـٰنُ مَآ أَكْفَرَهُ ﴿١٧﴾

17. Qutila al-insanu ma akfarahu
Be cursed (the disbelieving) man! How ungrateful he is!

		خَلَقَهُ	شَيْءٍ	أَيِّ	مِنْ
		khalaqahu	shay-in	ayyi	Min
		He created him	Thing	What	From

مِنْ أَيِّ شَيْءٍ خَلَقَهُ ۝

18. Min ayyi shay-in khalaqahu

From what thing did He create him?

		فَقَدَّرَهُ	خَلَقَهُ	نُطْفَةٍ	مِن
		Faqaddarahu	khalaqahu	nutfatin	Min
		Then set him in due proportion (proper form)	He created him	Semen	From

مِن نُّطْفَةٍ خَلَقَهُ فَقَدَّرَهُ ۝

19. Min nutfatin khalaqahu faqaddarahu

From *Nutfah* (male and female semen drops) He created him, and then set him in due proportion;

			يَسَّرَهُ	السَّبِيلَ	ثُمَّ
			yassarahu	alssabeela	Thumma
			He makes easy (for) him	The path	Then

ثُمَّ السَّبِيلَ يَسَّرَهُ ۝

20. Thumma alssabeela yassarahu

Then He makes the Path easy for him;

			فَأَقْبَرَهُ	أَمَاتَهُ	ثُمَّ
			faaqbarahu	amatahu	Thumma
			And puts him in his grave	He causes him to die	Then

ثُمَّ أَمَاتَهُ فَأَقْبَرَهُ ۝

21. Thumma amatahu faaqbarahu

Then He causes him to die, and puts him in his grave;

	أَنشَرَهُ	شَاءَ	إِذَا	ثُمَّ
	ansharahu	shaa	itha	Thumma
	He will resurrect him	He wills	When	Then

$$\text{ثُمَّ إِذَا شَاءَ أَنشَرَهُ ۝}$$

22. Thumma itha shaa ansharahu
Then, when it is His Will, He will resurrect him (again).

	أَمَرَهُ	مَا	يَقْضِ	لَمَّا	كَلَّا
	amarahu	ma	yaqdi	lamma	Kalla
	He commanded him	What	(has done) fulfilled	Not	Nay

$$\text{كَلَّا لَمَّا يَقْضِ مَا أَمَرَهُ ۝}$$

23. Kalla lamma yaqdi ma amarahu
Nay, but (man) has not done what He commanded him.

	طَعَامِهِ	إِلَى	الْإِنسَانُ	فَلْيَنظُرِ
	taAAamihi	ila	al-insanu	Falyanthuri
	His food	At	The man	Then let look

$$\text{فَلْيَنظُرِ ٱلْإِنسَٰنُ إِلَىٰ طَعَامِهِ ۝}$$

24. Falyanthuri al-insanu ila taAAamihi
Then let man look at his food,

	صَبًّا	الْمَاءَ	صَبَبْنَا	أَنَّا
	Sabban	almaa	sababna	Anna
	In Abundance	water	Pour forth	We

$$\text{أَنَّا صَبَبْنَا ٱلْمَاءَ صَبًّا ۝}$$

25. Anna sababna almaa sabban
That We pour forth water in abundance,

	شَقًّا	الْأَرْضَ	شَقَقْنَا	ثُمَّ
	shaqqan	al-arda	shaqaqna	Thumma

				In clefts	The Earth	we split	Then

$$ ثُمَّ شَقَقْنَا ٱلْأَرْضَ شَقًّا ۝ $$

26. Thumma shaqaqna al-arda shaqqan

And We split the earth in clefts,

			habban	feeha	Faanbatna
			The grain	Therein	And we cause to grow

$$ فَأَنۢبَتْنَا فِيهَا حَبًّا ۝ $$

27. Faanbatna feeha habban

And We cause therein the grain to grow,

			waqadban	WaAAinaban
			And clover plants	And grapes

$$ وَعِنَبًا وَقَضْبًا ۝ $$

28. WaAAinaban waqadban

And grapes and clover plants (i.e. green fodder for the cattle),

			wanakhlan	Wazaytoonan
			And date palms	And olives

$$ وَزَيْتُونًا وَنَخْلًا ۝ $$

29. Wazaytoonan wanakhlan

And olives and date-palms,

			ghulban	Wahada-iqa
			Dense with many trees	And gardens

وَحَدَآئِقَ غُلْبًا ۝

30. Wahada-iqa ghulban

And gardens, dense with many trees,

				waabban	Wafakihatan
				And herbage	And fruits

وَفَٰكِهَةً وَأَبًّا ۝

31. Wafakihatan waabban

And fruits and *Abba* (herbage, etc.),

			wali-anAAamikum	lakum	MataAAan
			And for your cattle	For you	To be a provision and benefit

مَّتَٰعًا لَّكُمْ وَلِأَنْعَٰمِكُمْ ۝

32. MataAAan lakum wali-anAAamikum

(To be) a provision and benefit for you and your cattle.

			alssakhkhatu	jaati	Fa-itha
			Deafing cry, Shout	(there) comes	Then when

فَإِذَا جَآءَتِ ٱلصَّآخَّةُ ۝

33. Fa-itha jaati alssakhkhatu

Then, when there comes *As-Sakhkhah* (the Day of Resurrection's second blowing of Trumpet),

akheehi	min	almaro	yafirru	Yawma
His brother	From	A man	Shall flee	That day

يَوْمَ يَفِرُّ ٱلْمَرْءُ مِنْ أَخِيهِ ﴿٣٤﴾

34. Yawma yafirru almaro min akheehi
That Day shall a man flee from his brother,

				وَأَبِيهِ	وَأُمِّهِ
				waabeehi	Waommihi
				And his father	And from his mother

وَأُمِّهِ وَأَبِيهِ ﴿٣٥﴾

35. Waommihi waabeehi
And from his mother and his father,

				وَبَنِيهِ	وَصَاحِبَتِهِ
				wabaneehi	Wasahibatihi
				And his children	And his wife

وَصَاحِبَتِهِ وَبَنِيهِ ﴿٣٦﴾

36. Wasahibatihi wabaneehi
And from his wife and his children.

يُغْنِيهِ	شَأْنٌ	يَوْمَئِذٍ	مِّنْهُمْ	امْرِئٍ	لِكُلِّ
yughneehi	sha/nun	yawma-ithin	minhum	imri-in	Likulli
It will make him careless (of Others)	(will be) enough concern	That day	Of them	Man	For every

لِكُلِّ ٱمْرِئٍ مِّنْهُمْ يَوْمَئِذٍ شَأْنٌ يُغْنِيهِ ﴿٣٧﴾

37. Likulli imri-in minhum yawma-ithin sha/nun yughneehi
Everyman, that Day, will have enough to make him careless of others.

			مُّسْفِرَةٌ	يَوْمَئِذٍ	وُجُوهٌ
			musfiratun	yawma-ithin	Wujoohun
			(will be) bright	That day	(some) faces

وُجُوهٌ يَوْمَئِذٍ مُّسْفِرَةٌ ﴿٣٨﴾

38. Wujoohun yawma-ithin musfiratun

Some faces that Day, will be bright (true believers of Islamic Monotheism).

				مُسْتَبْشِرَةٌ	ضَاحِكَةٌ
				mustabshiratun	Dahikatun
				Rejoicing at good news	Laughing

$$ ضَاحِكَةٌ مُّسْتَبْشِرَةٌ ۝ $$

39. Dahikatun mustabshiratun

Laughing, rejoicing at good news (of Paradise).

		غَبَرَةٌ	عَلَيْهَا	يَوْمَئِذٍ	وَوُجُوهٌ
		ghabaratun	AAalayha	yawma-ithin	Wawujoohun
		Will be dust	On them	That day	And (other) faces

$$ يَوْمَئِذٍ عَلَيْهَا غَبَرَةٌ ۝ $$

40. Wawujoohun yawma-ithin AAalayha ghabaratun

And other faces, that Day, will be dust-stained;

				قَتَرَةٌ	تَرْهَقُهَا
				qataratun	Tarhaquha
				Darkness	Will cover them

$$ تَرْهَقُهَا قَتَرَةٌ ۝ $$

41. Tarhaquha qataratun

Darkness will cover them,

		الْفَجَرَةُ	الْكَفَرَةُ	هُمُ	أُولَئِكَ
		alfajaratu	alkafaratu	humu	Ola-ika
		The evil-doer	The disbelievers	They (will be)	Such, those

$$ أُولَئِكَ هُمُ الْكَفَرَةُ الْفَجَرَةُ ۝ $$

42. Ola-ika humu alkafaratu alfajaratu

Such will be the *Kafarah* (disbelievers in Allah, in His Oneness, and in His Messenger Muhammad ﷺ, etc.), the *Fajarah* (wicked evil doers).

Surah # 81
AT-TAKWEER

Makkia

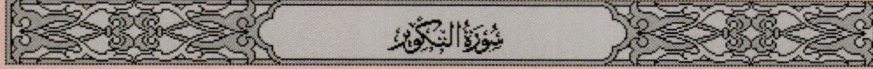

سُورَةُ التَّكْوِير

Verses 29
Section 1

بِسْمِ اللهِ الرَّحْمٰنِ الرَّحِيمِ

			كُوِّرَتْ	الشَّمْسُ	إِذَا
			kuwwirat	alshshamsu	Itha
			Would be round wound	The sun	When

﴿ إِذَا ٱلشَّمْسُ كُوِّرَتْ ۞ ١ ﴾

1. Itha alshshamsu kuwwirat
When the sun *Kuwwirat* (wound round and lost its light and is overthrown).

			انكَدَرَتْ	النُّجُومُ	وَإِذَا
			inkadarat	alnnujoomu	Wa-itha
			Shall fall	The starrs	And when

وَإِذَا ٱلنُّجُومُ ٱنكَدَرَتْ ۞ ٢

2. Wa-itha alnnujoomu inkadarat
And when the stars shall fall;

			سُيِّرَتْ	الْجِبَالُ	وَإِذَا
			suyyirat	aljibalu	Wa-itha
			Shall be moved away	The mountains	And when

وَإِذَا ٱلْجِبَالُ سُيِّرَتْ ۞ ٣

3. Wa-itha aljibalu suyyirat
And when the mountains shall made to pass away;

			AAuttilat	alAAisharu	Wa-itha
			Shall be neglected	The pregnant she camels	And when

وَإِذَا ٱلْعِشَارُ عُطِّلَتْ ﴿٤﴾

4. Wa-itha alAAisharu AAuttilat

And when the pregnant she-camels shall be neglected;

			hushirat	alwuhooshu	Wa-itha
			Shall be gathered together	The wild beast	And when

وَإِذَا ٱلْوُحُوشُ حُشِرَتْ ﴿٥﴾

5. Wa-itha alwuhooshu hushirat

And when the wild beasts shall be gathered together;

			sujjirat	albiharu	Wa-itha
			shall be made to over flow	the seas	And when

وَإِذَا ٱلْبِحَارُ سُجِّرَتْ ﴿٦﴾

6. Wa-itha albiharu sujjirat

And when the seas shall become as blazing Fire or shall overflow;

			zuwwijat	alnnufoosu	Wa-itha
			shall be joined	the souls	And when

وَإِذَا ٱلنُّفُوسُ زُوِّجَتْ ﴿٧﴾

7. Wa-itha alnnufoosu zuwwijat

And when the souls shall be joined with their bodies;

			سُئِلَتْ	الْمَوْءُۥدَةُ	وَإِذَا
			su-ilat	almawoodatu	Wa-itha
			Shall be questioned	The (female) infant buried alive	And when

وَإِذَا ٱلْمَوْءُۥدَةُ سُئِلَتْ ۝

8. Wa-itha almawoodatu su-ilat

And when the female (infant) buried alive (as the pagan Arabs used to do) shall be questioned.

			قُتِلَتْ	ذَنۢبٍ	بِأَيِّ
			qutilat	thanbin	Bi-ayyi
			She was killed	Sin	For what

بِأَيِّ ذَنۢبٍ قُتِلَتْ ۝

9. Bi-ayyi thanbin qutilat

For what sin she was killed?

			نُشِرَتْ	الصُّحُفُ	وَإِذَا
			nushirat	alssuhufu	Wa-itha
			Shall be laid open	the written pages (of deeds)	And when

وَإِذَا ٱلصُّحُفُ نُشِرَتْ ۝

10. Wa-itha alssuhufu nushirat

And when the written pages of deeds (good and bad) of every person shall be laid open;

			كُشِطَتْ	السَّمَاءُ	وَإِذَا
			kushitat	alssamao	Wa-itha
			Shall be stripped off	The heaven	And when

وَإِذَا ٱلسَّمَآءُ كُشِطَتْ ۝

11. Wa-itha alssamao kushitat

And when the heaven shall be stripped off and taken away from its place;

			سُعِّرَتْ	الْجَحِيمُ	وَإِذَا
			suAAAAirat	aljaheemu	Wa-itha
			Is kindled (to fierce heat)	Hell fire	And when

وَإِذَا الْجَحِيمُ سُعِّرَتْ ﴿١٢﴾

12. Wa-itha aljaheemu suAAAAirat

And when Hell-fire shall be kindled to fierce ablaze.

			أُزْلِفَتْ	الْجَنَّةُ	وَإِذَا
			ozlifat	aljannatu	Wa-itha
			Shall be brought near	Paradise	And when

وَإِذَا الْجَنَّةُ أُزْلِفَتْ ﴿١٣﴾

13. Wa-itha aljannatu ozlifat

And when Paradise shall be brought near,

	أَحْضَرَتْ	مَّا	نَفْسٌ	عَلِمَتْ
	ahdarat	ma	nafsun	AAalimat
	He has brought(of good and evil)	What	Every person	Will know

عَلِمَتْ نَفْسٌ مَّا أَحْضَرَتْ ﴿١٤﴾

14. AAalimat nafsun ma ahdarat

(Then) every person will know what he has brought (of good and evil).

		بِالْخُنَّسِ	أُقْسِمُ	فَلَا
		bialkhunnasi	oqsimu	Fala
		By the planets that recede	I swear	So verily

فَلَا أُقْسِمُ بِالْخُنَّسِ ﴿١٥﴾

15. Fala oqsimu bialkhunnasi

So verily, I swear by the planets that recede (i.e. disappear during the day and appear during the night).

				الْكُنَّسِ	الْجَوَارِ
				alkunnasi	Aljawari
				That move swiftly and hide themselves	And by the planets

$$ ٱلْجَوَارِ ٱلْكُنَّسِ ﴿١٦﴾ $$

16. Aljawari alkunnasi

And by the planets that move swiftly and hide themselves,

			عَسْعَسَ	إِذَا	وَاللَّيْلِ
			AAasAAasa	itha	Waallayli
			It departs	As	And by the night

$$ وَٱلَّيْلِ إِذَا عَسْعَسَ ﴿١٧﴾ $$

17. Waallayli itha AAasAAasa

And by the night as it departs;

			تَنَفَّسَ	إِذَا	وَالصُّبْحِ
			tanaffasa	itha	Waalssubhi
			It brightens	(when) as	And by the dawn

$$ وَٱلصُّبْحِ إِذَا تَنَفَّسَ ﴿١٨﴾ $$

18. Waalssubhi itha tanaffasa

And by the dawn as it brightens;

		كَرِيمٍ	رَسُولٍ	لَقَوْلُ	إِنَّهُ
		kareemin	Rasoolin	laqawlu	Innahu
		Most honourable	(of) a Messenger	(is) the word	Verily this

$$ إِنَّهُ لَقَوْلُ رَسُولٍ كَرِيمٍ ﴿١٩﴾ $$

19. Innahu laqawlu rasoolin kareemin

Verily, this is the Word (this Qur'an brought by) a most honourable messenger [Jibrael (Gabriel), from Allah to the Prophet Muhammad (ﷺ)].

مَكِين	الْعَرْش	ذِي	عِندَ	قُوَّةٍ	ذِي
makeenin	alAAarshi	thee	AAinda	quwwatin	Thee
Established	The Lord of the Throne		With		Mighty

ذِى قُوَّةٍ عِندَ ذِى ٱلْعَرْشِ مَكِينٍ ﴿٢٠﴾

20. Thee quwwatin AAinda thee alAAarshi makeenin

Owner of power, and high rank with (Allah) the Lord of the Throne,

			أَمِينٍ	ثَمَّ	مُطَاعٍ
			ameenin	thamma	MutaAAin
			Trustworthy	Then/and	Obeyed

مُّطَاعٍ ثَمَّ أَمِينٍ ﴿٢١﴾

21. MutaAAin thamma ameenin

21 Obeyed (by the angels), trustworthy there (in the heavens).

		بِمَجْنُونٍ	صَاحِبُكُم	وَمَا
		Bimajnoonin	sahibukum	Wama
		(is) a mad man	Your companion	And not

وَمَا صَاحِبُكُم بِمَجْنُونٍ ﴿٢٢﴾

22. Wama sahibukum bimajnoonin

22 And (O people) your companion (Muhammad (ﷺ)) is not a madman;

الْمُبِين	بِالْأُفُقِ	رَآهُ	وَلَقَدْ
almubeeni	Bialofuqi	raahu	Walaqad
Clear	In the Horizon	He saw him	And indeed

وَلَقَدْ رَءَاهُ بِٱلْأُفُقِ ٱلْمُبِينِ ﴿٢٣﴾

23. Walaqad raahu bialofuqi almubeeni

23 And indeed he (Muhammad (ﷺ)) saw him [Jibrael (Gabriel)] in the clear horizon (towards the east).

بِضَنِينٍ	الْغَيْب	عَلَى	هُوَ	وَمَا
bidaneenin	alghaybi	AAala	huwa	Wama

	Withholds	The unseen	(on)	He	And not

وَمَا هُوَ عَلَى ٱلْغَيْبِ بِضَنِينٍ ۝

24. Wama huwa AAala alghaybi bidaneenin

24 And he (Muhammad (ﷺ)) withholds not a knowledge of the unseen.

رَجِيمٌ	شَيْطَانٍ	بِقَوْلِ	هُوَ	وَمَا
rajeemin	shaytanin	biqawli	huwa	Wama
Outcast	(of) satan	Thw word	It (is)	And not

وَمَا هُوَ بِقَوْلِ شَيْطَانٍ رَّجِيمٍ ۝

25. Wama huwa biqawli shaytanin rajeemin

25 And it (the Qur'an) is not the word of the outcast *Shaitan* (Satan).

			تَذْهَبُونَ	فَأَيْنَ
			tathhaboona	Faayna
			You are going	Then where

فَأَيْنَ تَذْهَبُونَ ۝

26. Faayna tathhaboona

26 Then where are you going?

لِّلْعَالَمِينَ	ذِكْرٌ	إِلَّا	هُوَ	إِنْ
lilAAalameena	thikrun	illa	Huwa	In
To the worlds	A reminder	But	This (is)	Not

إِنْ هُوَ إِلَّا ذِكْرٌ لِّلْعَالَمِينَ ۝

27. In huwa illa thikrun lilAAalameena

27 Verily, this (the Qur'an) is no less than a Reminder to (all) the *'Alamin* (mankind and jinns).

يَسْتَقِيمَ	أَن	مِنكُمْ	شَاءَ	لِمَن
yastaqeema	an	minkum	shaa	Liman
Walk straight	To	Among you	Who wills	To whomsoever

41

$$\text{لِمَن شَآءَ مِنكُمْ أَن يَسْتَقِيمَ ﴿٢٨﴾}$$

28. Liman shaa minkum an yastaqeema

28 To whomsoever among you who wills to walk straight,

وَمَا	تَشَآءُونَ	إِلَّا	أَن	يَشَآء	ٱللَّهُ
Wama	tashaoona	illa	an	Yashaa	Allahu
And not	You can will	Unless	That	Wills	Allah

رَبُّ	ٱلْعَالَمِينَ				
rabbu	alAAalameena				
The Lord	(of) the worlds				

$$\text{وَمَا تَشَآءُونَ إِلَّا أَن يَشَآءَ ٱللَّهُ رَبُّ ٱلْعَٰلَمِينَ ﴿٢٩﴾}$$

29. Wama tashaoona illa an yashaa Allahu rabbu alAAalameena

29 And you will not, unless (it be) that Allah wills, the Lord of the *'Alamin* (mankind, jinns and all that exists).

Surah # 82
AL-INFITAR

Makkia

$$\text{سُورَةُ الاِنفِطَارِ}$$

$$\text{بِسْمِ ٱللَّهِ ٱلرَّحْمَٰنِ ٱلرَّحِيمِ}$$

إِذَا	السَّمَاء	انفَطَرَتْ			
Itha	alssamao	infatarat			
When	The heavens	Is cleft asunder			

$$\text{إِذَا ٱلسَّمَآءُ ٱنفَطَرَتْ ﴿١﴾}$$

1. Itha alssamao infatarat

1 When the heaven is cleft asunder.

وَإِذَا	الْكَوَاكِبُ	انتَثَرَتْ			
waitha	alkawakibu	intatharat			

42

			intatharat	alkawakibu	Wa-itha
			Have scattered	The stars	And when

وَإِذَا ٱلْكَوَاكِبُ ٱنتَثَرَتْ ﴿٢﴾

2. Wa-itha alkawakibu intatharat

2 And when the stars have fallen and scattered;

		فُجِّرَتْ	الْبِحَارُ	وَإِذَا
		fujjirat	albiharu	Wa-itha
		Are burst forth	The oceans	And when

وَإِذَا ٱلْبِحَارُ فُجِّرَتْ ﴿٣﴾

3. Wa-itha albiharu fujjirat

3 And when the seas are burst forth;

		بُعْثِرَتْ	الْقُبُورُ	وَإِذَا
		buAAthirat	alqubooru	Wa-itha
		Are turned upside down	The graves	And when

وَإِذَا ٱلْقُبُورُ بُعْثِرَتْ ﴿٤﴾

4. Wa-itha alqubooru buAAthirat

4 And when the graves are turned upside down (and they bring out their contents)

وَأَخَّرَتْ	قَدَّمَتْ	مَّا	نَفْسٌ	عَلِمَتْ
waakhkharat	qaddamat	ma	nafsun	AAalimat
And left behind	It has sent forward	What	(every) Soul	Will know

عَلِمَتْ نَفْسٌ مَّا قَدَّمَتْ وَأَخَّرَتْ ﴿٥﴾

5. AAalimat nafsun ma qaddamat waakhkharat

5 (Then) a person will know what he has sent forward and (what he has) left behind (of good or bad deeds).

الْكَرِيمِ	بِرَبِّكَ	غَرَّكَ	مَا	الْإِنسَانُ	يَاأَيُّهَا
birabbika	gharraka	ma	al-insanu	ayyuha	Ya
The most generous	About your Lord	Made you careless	What	Man	O
					alkareemi

يَـٰٓأَيُّهَا ٱلْإِنسَـٰنُ مَا غَرَّكَ بِرَبِّكَ ٱلْكَرِيمِ ۝

6. Ya ayyuha al-insanu ma gharraka birabbika alkareemi

6 O man! What has made you careless concerning your Lord, the Most Generous?

		فَعَدَلَكَ	فَسَوَّىٰكَ	خَلَقَكَ	ٱلَّذِى
		faAAadalaka	fasawwaka	khalaqaka	Allathee
		And gave you (due) proportions	Faishoned you (perfectly)	created you	Who

ٱلَّذِى خَلَقَكَ فَسَوَّىٰكَ فَعَدَلَكَ ۝

7. Allathee khalaqaka fasawwaka faAAadalaka

7 Who created you, fashioned you perfectly, and gave you due proportion;

رَكَّبَكَ	شَاءَ	مَّا	صُورَةٍ	أَيِّ	فِى
Rakkabaka	shaa	ma	sooratin	ayyi	Fee
He put you together	He willed	That	Form	Whatever	In

فِى أَيِّ صُورَةٍ مَّا شَاءَ رَكَّبَكَ ۝

8. Fee ayyi sooratin ma shaa rakkabaka

8 In whatever form He willed, He put you together.

		بِٱلدِّينِ	تُكَذِّبُونَ	بَلْ	كَلَّا
		bialddeeni	tukaththiboona	bal	Kalla
		The judgement	You denny / belie	But	Nay

كَلَّا بَلْ تُكَذِّبُونَ بِٱلدِّينِ ۝

9. Kalla bal tukaththiboona bialddeeni

9 Nay! But you deny the Recompense (reward for good deeds and punishment for evil deeds).

		لَحَافِظِينَ	عَلَيْكُمْ	وَإِنَّ
		lahafitheena	AAalaykum	Wa-inna
		(are) vigilants	Over you	But verily

وَإِنَّ عَلَيْكُمْ لَحَافِظِينَ ﴿١٠﴾

10. Wa-inna AAalaykum lahafitheena
10 But verily, over you (are appointed angels in charge of mankind) to watch you,

				katibeena	Kiraman
				Writing down	Honourable

كِرَامًا كَتِبِينَ ﴿١١﴾

11. Kiraman katibeena
11 *Kiraman* (honourable) *Katibin* writing down (your deeds),

			tafAAaloona	ma	YaAAlamoona
			You do	What	They know

يَعْلَمُونَ مَا تَفْعَلُونَ ﴿١٢﴾

12. YaAAlamoona ma tafAAaloona
12 They know all that you do.

		naAAeemin	lafee	al-abrara	Inna
		Delight	(will be) in	The righteous	Verily

إِنَّ ٱلْأَبْرَارَ لَفِى نَعِيمٍ ﴿١٣﴾

13. Inna al-abrara lafee naAAeemin
13 Verily, the *Abrar* (pious and righteous) will be in delight (Paradise);

		jaheemin	lafee	alfujjara	Wa-inna
		Fire	(will be) in	The wicked	And verily

وَإِنَّ ٱلْفُجَّارَ لَفِى جَحِيمٍ ﴿١٤﴾

14. Wa-inna alfujjara lafee jaheemin
14 And verily, the *Fujjar* (the wicked, disbelievers, sinners and evil-doers) will be in the

blazing Fire (Hell),

			لدِّينِ	يَوْمَ	يَصْلَوْنَهَا
			alddeeni	yawma	Yaslawnaha
			(of) Recomoense	on the day	They will burn in it

يَصْلَوْنَهَا يَوْمَ ٱلدِّينِ ﴿١٥﴾

15. Yaslawnaha yawma alddeeni

15 In which they will enter, and taste its burning flame on the Day of Recompense,

		بِغَائِبِينَ	عَنْهَا	هُمْ	وَمَا
		bigha-ibeena	AAanha	hum	Wama
		(Will be) Absent	Therefrom	They	And not

وَمَا هُمْ عَنْهَا بِغَآئِبِينَ ﴿١٦﴾

16. Wama hum AAanha bigha-ibeena

16 And they (Al-Fujjar) will not be absent therefrom (i.e. will not go out from the Hell).

	لدِّينِ	يَوْمُ	مَا	أَدْرَاكَ	وَمَا
	alddeeni	yawmu	ma	adraka	Wama
	Of the Recompense (is)	The day	What	Will make you know	And what

وَمَآ أَدْرَىٰكَ مَا يَوْمُ ٱلدِّينِ ﴿١٧﴾

17. Wama adraka ma yawmu alddeeni

17 And what will make you know what the Day of Recompense is?

الدِّينِ	يَوْمُ	مَا	أَدْرَاكَ	مَا	ثُمَّ
alddeeni	yawmu	ma	adraka	ma	Thumma
(of) Recompense (is)	The day	What	Will make you know	What	Then

ثُمَّ مَآ أَدْرَىٰكَ مَا يَوْمُ ٱلدِّينِ ﴿١٨﴾

18. Thumma ma adraka ma yawmu alddeeni

18 Again, what will make you know what the Day of Recompense is?

46

شَيْئًا	لِّنَفْسٍ	نَفْسٌ	تَمْلِكُ	لَا	يَوْمَ
shay-an	linafsin	nafsun	tamliku	la	Yawma
Any thing	For any soul	A soul (person)	Shall have power	Not	The day (when)

			لِلَّهِ	يَوْمَئِذٍ	وَٱلْأَمْرُ
			lillahi	yawma-ithin	Waal-amru
			Will be with Allah	That day	And the decision

يَوْمَ لَا تَمْلِكُ نَفْسٌ لِّنَفْسٍ شَيْئًا ۖ وَٱلْأَمْرُ يَوْمَئِذٍ لِّلَّهِ ﴿١٩﴾

19. Yawma la tamliku nafsun linafsin shay-an waal-amru yawma-ithin lillahi

19 (It will be) the Day when no person shall have power (to do) anything for another, and the Decision, that Day, will be (wholly) with Allah.

Surah # 83
AL-MUTAFFIFEEN

Makkia

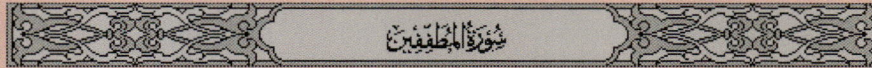

Verses 36

Sections 1

بِسْمِ ٱللَّهِ ٱلرَّحْمَٰنِ ٱلرَّحِيمِ

				لِّلْمُطَفِّفِينَ	وَيْلٌ
				lilmutaffifeena	Waylun
				Th Al-Mutaffifin (those who give less in measure and weight)	Woe

﴿ وَيْلٌ لِّلْمُطَفِّفِينَ ﴿١﴾

1. Waylun lilmutaffifeena

1 Woe to *Al-Mutaffifin* [those who give less in measure and weight (decrease the rights of others)],

الَّذِينَ	إِذَا	اكْتَالُواْ	عَلَى	النَّاسِ	يَسْتَوْفُونَ
Allatheena	itha	iktaloo	AAala	alnnasi	yastawfoona
Those who	When	They receive by measure	From (on)	Men	They demand full measure

ٱلَّذِينَ إِذَا ٱكْتَالُواْ عَلَى ٱلنَّاسِ يَسْتَوْفُونَ ۝

2. Allatheena itha iktaloo AAala alnnasi yastawfoona

2 Those who, when they have to receive by measure from men, demand full measure,

وَإِذَا	كَالُوهُمْ	أَو	وَّزَنُوهُمْ	يُخْسِرُونَ
Wa-itha	kaloohum	aw	wazanoohum	yukhsiroona
And when	They give by measure to them	Or	They give by weight to them	They give less than due

وَإِذَا كَالُوهُمْ أَوْ وَّزَنُوهُمْ يُخْسِرُونَ ۝

3. Wa-itha kaloohum aw wazanoohum yukhsiroona

3 And when they have to give by measure or weight to men, give less than due.

أَلَا	يَظُنُّ	أُوْلَئِكَ	أَنَّهُم	مَّبْعُوثُونَ
Ala	yathunnu	ola-ika	annahum	mabAAoothoona
Do not	Think	They	That they	(will be) resurrected

أَلَا يَظُنُّ أُوْلَئِكَ أَنَّهُم مَّبْعُوثُونَ ۝

4. Ala yathunnu ola-ika annahum mabAAoothoona

4 Think they not that they will be resurrected (for reckoning),

				لِيَوْمٍ	عَظِيمٍ
				Liyawmin	AAatheemin
				On a day	Great

لِيَوْمٍ عَظِيمٍ ۝

5. Liyawmin AAatheemin

5 On a Great Day,

	الْعَالَمِينَ	لِرَبِّ	النَّاسُ	يَقُومُ	يَوْمَ
	alAAalameena	lirabbi	alnnasu	Yaqoomu	Yawma
	(of) the worlds	Before the Lord	Mankind	Will stand	The day (when)

يَوْمَ يَقُومُ ٱلنَّاسُ لِرَبِّ ٱلْعَٰلَمِينَ ۝

6. Yawma yaqoomu alnnasu lirabbi alAAalameena

6 The Day when (all) mankind will stand before the Lord of the 'Alamin (mankind, jinns and all that exists)?

سِجِّينٍ	لَفِي	الْفُجَّارِ	كِتَابَ	إِنَّ	كَلَّا
sijjeenin	lafee	alfujjari	kitaba	inna	Kalla
Sijjin	(is) in	(of) the sinners, wicked	Record	Truly	Nay

كَلَّآ إِنَّ كِتَٰبَ ٱلْفُجَّارِ لَفِى سِجِّينٍ ۝

7. Kalla inna kitaba alfujjari lafee sijjeenin

7 Nay! Truly, the Record (writing of the deeds) of the *Fujjar* (disbelievers, sinners, evil-doers and wicked) is (preserved) in *Sijjin*.

		سِجِّينٌ	مَا	أَدْرَاكَ	وَمَا
		sijjeenun	ma	adraka	Wama
		(is) sijjin	What	Will make you know	And what

وَمَآ أَدْرَىٰكَ مَا سِجِّينٌ ۝

8. Wama adraka ma sijjeenun

8 And what will make you know what *Sijjin* is?

				مَّرْقُومٌ	كِتَابٌ
				marqoomun	Kitabun
				Inscribed	A register

كِتَٰبٌ مَّرْقُومٌ ۝

9. Kitabun marqoomun

9 A Register inscribed.

			لِّلْمُكَذِّبِينَ	يَوْمَئِذٍ	وَيْلٌ
			lilmukaththib eena	yawma-ithin	Waylun
			To those who deny	That day	Woe

وَيْلٌ يَوْمَئِذٍ لِّلْمُكَذِّبِينَ ۝

10. Waylun yawma-ithin lilmukaththibeena

10 Woe, that Day, to those who deny [(Allah, His Angels, His Books, His Messengers, the Day of Resurrection, and *Al-Qadar* (Divine Preordainments)].

		الدِّينِ	بِيَوْمِ	يُكَذِّبُونَ	الَّذِينَ
		alddeeni	biyawmi	yukaththiboo na	Allatheena
		(of) Recompense	The day	Who deny	Those

الَّذِينَ يُكَذِّبُونَ بِيَوْمِ الدِّينِ ۝

11. Allatheena yukaththiboona biyawmi alddeeni

11 Those who deny the Day of Recompense.

مُعْتَدٍ	كُلُّ	إِلَّا	بِهِ	يُكَذِّبُ	وَمَا
muAAtadin	kullu	illa	bihi	yukaththibu	Wama
Transgressor beyond bounds	Every	Except	It	Can deny	And none
				أَثِيمٍ	
				atheemin	
				Sinner	

وَمَا يُكَذِّبُ بِهِ إِلَّا كُلُّ مُعْتَدٍ أَثِيمٍ ۝

12. Wama yukaththibu bihi illa kullu muAAtadin atheemin

12 And none can deny it except every transgressor beyond bounds, (in disbelief, oppression and disobedience of Allah, the sinner!)

أَسَاطِيرُ	قَالَ	آيَاتُنَا	عَلَيْهِ	تُتْلَى	إِذَا
asateeru	qala	ayatuna	AAalayhi	tutla	Itha
Tales	He says	Our verses	To him	Are recieted	When
					الْأَوَّلِينَ

					al-awwaleena
					(of) the Ancients

إِذَا تُتْلَىٰ عَلَيْهِ ءَايَٰتُنَا قَالَ أَسَٰطِيرُ ٱلْأَوَّلِينَ ﴿١٣﴾

13. Itha tutla AAalayhi ayatuna qala asateeru al-awwaleena

13 When Our Verses (of the Qur'an) are recited to him he says: "Tales of the ancients!"

مَّا	قُلُوبِهِم	عَلَىٰ	رَانَ	بَلْ	كَلَّا
ma	quloobihim	AAala	rana	bal	Kalla
Which	Their hearts	On	(is) Ran (covering of sins and evil deeds)	But	Nay

			يَكْسِبُونَ	كَانُوا	
			yaksiboona	Kanoo	
			They used to earn	were	

كَلَّا بَلْ رَانَ عَلَىٰ قُلُوبِهِم مَّا كَانُوا۟ يَكْسِبُونَ ﴿١٤﴾

14. Kalla bal rana AAala quloobihim ma kanoo yaksiboona

14 Nay! But on their hearts is the *Ran* (covering of sins and evil deeds) which they used to earn.

لَّمَحْجُوبُونَ	يَوْمَئِذٍ	رَّبِّهِمْ	عَن	إِنَّهُمْ	كَلَّا
lamahjooboona	yawma-ithin	rabbihim	AAan	innahum	Kalla
(will be) veiled	That day	Their Lord	From	Surely they	Nay

كَلَّا إِنَّهُمْ عَن رَّبِّهِمْ يَوْمَئِذٍ لَّمَحْجُوبُونَ ﴿١٥﴾

15. Kalla innahum AAan rabbihim yawma-ithin lamahjooboona

15 Nay! Surely, they (evil-doers) will be veiled from seeing their Lord that Day.

			الْجَحِيمِ	لَصَالُوا	إِنَّهُمْ	ثُمَّ
			aljaheemi	lasaloo	innahum	Thumma
			(in) the hell	Indeed will burn	Verily they	Then

ثُمَّ إِنَّهُمْ لَصَالُوا۟ ٱلْجَحِيمِ ﴿١٦﴾

16. Thumma innahum lasaloo aljaheemi

16 Then, verily they will indeed enter and taste the burning flame of Hell.

بِهِ	كُنتُم	الَّذِي	هَذَا	يُقَالُ	ثُمَّ
bihi	kuntum	allathee	hatha	yuqalu	Thumma
(it)	You used to	(s) which	This	It will be said	Then
					تُكَذِّبُونَ
					tukaththiboona
					Deny

ثُمَّ يُقَالُ هَـٰذَا ٱلَّذِى كُنتُم بِهِۦ تُكَذِّبُونَ ﴿١٧﴾

17. Thumma yuqalu hatha allathee kuntum bihi tukaththiboona

17 Then, it will be said to them: "This is what you used to deny!"

عِلِّيِّينَ	لَفِي	الْأَبْرَارِ	كِتَابَ	إِنَّ	كَلَّا
AAilliyyeena	lafee	al-abrari	kitaba	inna	Kalla
Illiyyin	(will be) indeed in	(of) the righteous	Record	Verily	Nay

كَلَّآ إِنَّ كِتَـٰبَ ٱلْأَبْرَارِ لَفِى عِلِّيِّينَ ﴿١٨﴾

18. Kalla inna kitaba al-abrari lafee AAilliyyeena

18 Nay! Verily, the Record (writing of the deeds) of *Al-Abrar* (the pious who fear Allah and avoid evil), is (preserved) in *'Illiyyun*.

		عِلِّيُّونَ	مَا	أَدْرَاكَ	وَمَا
		AAilliyyoona	ma	adraka	Wama
		Illiyyun	What	Will make you know	And what

وَمَآ أَدْرَىٰكَ مَا عِلِّيُّونَ ﴿١٩﴾

19. Wama adraka ma AAilliyyoona

19 And what will make you know what *'Illiyyun* is?

				مَّرْقُومٌ	كِتَابٌ
				marqoomun	Kitabun
				Inscribed	A register

كِتَٰبٌ مَّرْقُومٌ ﴿٢٠﴾

20. Kitabun marqoomun

20 A Register inscribed.

				الْمُقَرَّبُونَ	يَشْهَدُهُ
				almuqarraboona	Yashhaduhu
				Those nearest (to Allah)	To which bear witness

يَشْهَدُهُ ٱلْمُقَرَّبُونَ ﴿٢١﴾

21. Yashhaduhu almuqarraboona

21 To which bear witness those nearest (to Allah, i.e. the angels).

		نَعِيمٍ	لَفِي	الْأَبْرَارَ	إِنَّ
		naAAeemin	lafee	al-abrara	Inna
		Delight	(will be) in	The Righteous	Verily

إِنَّ ٱلْأَبْرَارَ لَفِى نَعِيمٍ ﴿٢٢﴾

22. Inna al-abrara lafee naAAeemin

22 Verily, *Al-Abrar* (the pious who fear Allah and avoid evil) will be in delight (Paradise).

		يَنظُرُونَ	الْأَرَائِكِ	عَلَى
		yanthuroona	al-ara-iki	AAala
		Looking	Thornes	On

عَلَى ٱلْأَرَآئِكِ يَنظُرُونَ ﴿٢٣﴾

23. AAala al-ara-iki yanthuroona

23 On thrones, looking (at all things).

النَّعِيمِ	نَضْرَةَ	وُجُوهِهِمْ	فِي	تَعْرِفُ
alnnaAAeemi	nadrata	wujoohihim	fee	TaAArifu
(of) delight	The brightness	Their faces	In	You will recognise

تَعْرِفُ فِي وُجُوهِهِمْ نَضْرَةَ ٱلنَّعِيمِ ﴿٢٤﴾

24. TaAArifu fee wujoohihim nadrata alnnaAAeemi

24 You will recognise in their faces the brightness of delight.

		مَّخْتُومٍ	رَّحِيقٍ	مِن	يُسْقَوْنَ
		makhtoomin	raheeqin	min	Yusqawna
		Sealed	Pure wine	from/of	They wll be given to drink

يُسْقَوْنَ مِن رَّحِيقٍ مَّخْتُومٍ ﴿٢٥﴾

25. Yusqawna min raheeqin makhtoomin

25 They will be given to drink pure sealed wine.

ٱلْمُتَنَافِسُونَ	فَلْيَتَنَافَسِ	ذَٰلِكَ	وَفِي	مِسْكٌ	خِتَامُهُ
almutanafisoona	falyatanafasi	Thalika	wafee	miskun	Khitamuhu
Those who want to strive	Let srive	This	And for	(will be) smell of Musk	The last thereof

خِتَامُهُ مِسْكٌ وَفِي ذَٰلِكَ فَلْيَتَنَافَسِ ٱلْمُتَنَافِسُونَ ﴿٢٦﴾

26. Khitamuhu miskun wafee thalika falyatanafasi almutanafisoona

26 The last thereof (that wine) will be the smell of musk, and for this let (all) those strive who want to strive (i.e. hasten earnestly to the obedience of Allah).

		تَسْنِيمٍ	مِن	وَمِزَاجُهُ
		tasneemin	min	Wamizajuhu
		Tasnim	From	And its mixture (will Be)

وَمِزَاجُهُ مِن تَسْنِيمٍ ﴿٢٧﴾

27. Wamizajuhu min tasneemin

27 It (that wine) will be mixed with *Tasnim*.

		ٱلْمُقَرَّبُونَ	بِهَا	يَشْرَبُ	عَيْنًا
		almuqarraboona	biha	yashrabu	AAaynan
		Those nearest	Whereof	Will drink	A spring

54

			to Allah		

عَيْنًا يَشْرَبُ بِهَا ٱلْمُقَرَّبُونَ ۝

28. AAaynan yashrabu biha almuqarraboona

28 A spring whereof drink those nearest to Allah.

الَّذِينَ	مِنَ	كَانُوا	أَجْرَمُوا	الَّذِينَ	إِنَّ
allatheena	mina	kanoo	ajramoo	allatheena	Inna
Those who	At	They used to	Who commited crimes	Those	Verily

			آمَنُوا	يَضْحَكُونَ	
			yadhakoona	amanoo	
			Laugh	Believed	

إِنَّ ٱلَّذِينَ أَجْرَمُوا كَانُوا مِنَ ٱلَّذِينَ ءَامَنُوا يَضْحَكُونَ ۝

29. Inna allatheena ajramoo kanoo mina allatheena amanoo yadhakoona

29 Verily! (During the worldly life) those who committed crimes used to laugh at those who believed.

		يَتَغَامَزُونَ	بِهِمْ	مَرُّوا	وَإِذَا
		yataghamazoona	bihim	marroo	Wa-itha
		They used to wink one to another	By them	They passed	And whenever

وَإِذَا مَرُّوا بِهِمْ يَتَغَامَزُونَ ۝

30. Wa-itha marroo bihim yataghamazoona

30 And whenever they passed by them, used to wink one to another (in mockery);

فَكِهِينَ	انقَلَبُوا	أَهْلِهِمُ	إِلَى	انقَلَبُوا	وَإِذَا
fakiheena	inqalaboo	ahlihimu	ila	inqalaboo	Wa-itha
Jesting	They would return	Their own people	To	They returned	And when

وَإِذَا ٱنقَلَبُوا إِلَى أَهْلِهِمُ ٱنقَلَبُوا فَكِهِينَ ۝

31. Wa-itha inqalaboo ila ahlihimu inqalaboo fakiheena

31 And when they returned to their own people, they would return jesting;

وَإِذَا	رَأَوْهُمْ	قَالُوا	إِنَّ	هَٰؤُلَاءِ	لَضَالُّونَ
Wa-itha	raawhum	qaloo	inna	haola-i	ladalloona
And when	They saw them	They said	Verily	These	Indeed have gone astray

وَإِذَا رَأَوْهُمْ قَالُوا إِنَّ هَٰؤُلَاءِ لَضَالُّونَ ۝

32. Wa-itha raawhum qaloo inna haola-i ladalloona

32 And when they saw them, they said: "Verily! These have indeed gone astray!"

وَمَا	أُرْسِلُوا	عَلَيْهِمْ	حَافِظِينَ		
Wama	orsiloo	AAalayhim	hafitheena		
But not	They had been sent	Over them	(as) watchers		

وَمَا أُرْسِلُوا عَلَيْهِمْ حَافِظِينَ ۝

33. Wama orsiloo AAalayhim hafitheena

33 But they (disbelievers, sinners) had not been sent as watchers over them (the believers).

فَالْيَوْمَ	الَّذِينَ	آمَنُوا	مِنَ	الْكُفَّارِ	يَضْحَكُونَ
Faalyawma	allatheena	amanoo	mina	alkuffari	yadhakoona
But this day	Those	Who believe	At	The disbelievers	Will laugh

فَالْيَوْمَ الَّذِينَ آمَنُوا مِنَ الْكُفَّارِ يَضْحَكُونَ ۝

34. Faalyawma allatheena amanoo mina alkuffari yadhakoona

34 But this Day (the Day of Resurrection) those who believe will laugh at the disbelievers

عَلَى	الْأَرَائِكِ	يَنظُرُونَ			
AAala	al-ara-iki	yanthuroona			
On	Thrones	Looking			

عَلَى الْأَرَائِكِ يَنظُرُونَ ۝

35. AAala al-ara-iki yanthuroona

35 On (high) thrones, looking (at all things).

يَفْعَلُونَ	كَانُوا	مَا	الْكُفَّارُ	ثُوِّبَ	هَلْ
yafAAaloona	kanoo	ma	alkuffaru	thuwwiba	Hal
Do	They used to	For what	The disbelievers	Paid	Are not

هَلْ ثُوِّبَ ٱلْكُفَّارُ مَا كَانُوٓاْ يَفْعَلُونَ ۝

36. Hal thuwwiba alkuffaru ma kanoo yafAAaloona

36 Are not the disbelievers paid (fully) for what they used to do?

Surah # 84
AL-INSHIQAQ

Makkia

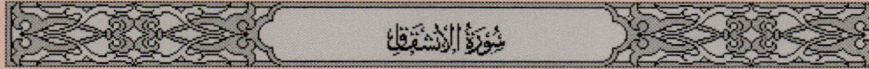

Verses 25
Sections 1

بِسْمِ ٱللَّهِ ٱلرَّحْمَٰنِ ٱلرَّحِيمِ

			انشَقَّتْ	السَّمَاءُ	إِذَا
			inshaqqat	alssamao	Itha
			Is split under	The Heaven	When

إِذَا ٱلسَّمَآءُ ٱنشَقَّتْ ۝

1. Itha alssamao inshaqqat

1 When the heaven is split asunder,

			وَحُقَّتْ	لِرَبِّهَا	وَأَذِنَتْ
			wahuqqat	lirabbiha	Waathinat
			And it must do so	To its Lord	And listens

وَأَذِنَتْ لِرَبِّهَا وَحُقَّتْ ۝

2. Waathinat lirabbiha wahuqqat

2 And listens and obeys its Lord, and it must do so;

			مُدَّتْ	الْأَرْضُ	وَإِذَا
			muddat	al-ardu	Wa-itha
			Is streached forth	The earth	And when

وَإِذَا ٱلْأَرْضُ مُدَّتْ ۝

3. Wa-itha al-ardu muddat
3 And when the earth is stretched forth,

		وَتَخَلَّتْ	فِيهَا	مَا	وَأَلْقَتْ
		watakhallat	feeha	ma	Waalqat
		And became empty	(was) in it	All that	And cast out

وَأَلْقَتْ مَا فِيهَا وَتَخَلَّتْ ۝

4. Waalqat ma feeha watakhallat
4 And has cast out all that was in it and became empty,

		وَحُقَّتْ	لِرَبِّهَا	وَأَذِنَتْ
		wahuqqat	lirabbiha	Waathinat
		And it must do so	Its Lord	And listens to and obeys

وَأَذِنَتْ لِرَبِّهَا وَحُقَّتْ ۝

5. Waathinat lirabbiha wahuqqat
5 And listens and obeys its Lord, and it must do so;

إِلَى	كَادِحٌ	إِنَّكَ	الْإِنسَانُ	أَيُّهَا	يَا
ila	kadihun	innaka	al-insanu	ayyuha	Ya
Towards	Are exerting	Verily you	Man	you	O!

		فَمُلَاقِيهِ	كَدْحًا	رَبِّكَ
		famulaqeehi	kadhan	rabbika
		(you) will meet him	Very hard	Your Lord

يَٰأَيُّهَا ٱلْإِنسَٰنُ إِنَّكَ كَادِحٌ إِلَىٰ رَبِّكَ كَدْحًا فَمُلَٰقِيهِ ۝

6. Ya ayyuha al-insanu innaka kadihun ila rabbika kadhan famulaqeehi

6 O man! Verily, you are returning towards your Lord with your deeds and actions (good or bad), a sure returning, so you will meet (i.e. the results of your deeds which you did).

فَأَمَّا	مَنْ	أُوتِيَ	كِتَابَهُ	بِيَمِينِهِ
Faama	man	ootiya	kitabahu	biyameenih**i**
Then as for	Him who	Will be given	His record	In his right hand

فَأَمَّا مَنْ أُوتِيَ كِتَابَهُ بِيَمِينِهِ ۝

7. Faam**a** man ootiya kit**a**bahu biyameenih**i**

7 Then, as for him who will be given his Record in his right hand,

فَسَوْفَ	يُحَاسَبُ	حِسَابًا	يَسِيرًا
Fasawfa	yuhasabu	hisaban	yaseer**a**n
Surely will	He be reckoned	A reckoning	Easy

فَسَوْفَ تُحَاسَبُ حِسَابًا يَسِيرًا ۝

8. Fasawfa yuhasabu hi**s**aban yaseer**a**n

8 He surely will receive an easy reckoning,

وَيَنقَلِبُ	إِلَى	أَهْلِهِ	مَسْرُورًا
Wayanqalibu	il**a**	ahlihi	masroor**a**n
And will return	To	His family	Happy , glad

وَيَنقَلِبُ إِلَى أَهْلِهِ مَسْرُورًا ۝

9. Wayanqalibu il**a** ahlihi masroor**a**n

9 And will return to his family in joy!

وَأَمَّا	مَنْ	أُوتِيَ	كِتَابَهُ	وَرَاءَ	ظَهْرِهِ
Waamm**a**	man	ootiya	Kit**a**bahu	war**a**a	*th*ahrihi
But	Whosoever	Is given	His record	Behind	His back

وَأَمَّا مَنْ أُوتِيَ كِتَابَهُ وَرَاءَ ظَهْرِهِ ۝

10. Waamm**a** man ootiya ki**t**abahu war**a**a *th*ahrihi

10 But whosoever is given his Record behind his back,

			ثُبُورًا	يَدْعُو	فَسَوْفَ
			thuboor**a**n	yadAAoo	Fasawfa
			(For Destruction)	He invoke	Will

فَسَوْفَ يَدْعُواْ ثُبُورًا ۝

11. Fasawfa yadAAoo thuboor**a**n

11 He will invoke (his) destruction,

			سَعِيرًا	وَيَصْلَى
			saAAeer**a**n	Waya**s**la
			In a blazing fire	And burn/enter

وَيَصْلَى سَعِيرًا ۝

12. Waya**s**la saAAeer**a**n

12 And shall enter a blazing Fire, and made to taste its burning.

مَسْرُورًا	أَهْلِهِ	فِي	كَانَ	إِنَّهُ
masroor**a**n	ahlihi	fee	k**a**na	Innahu
In joy	His people	Among	Was	Verily He

إِنَّهُ كَانَ فِي أَهْلِهِ مَسْرُورًا ۝

13. Innahu k**a**na fee ahlihi masroor**a**n

13 Verily, he was among his people in joy!

يَحُورَ	لَّن	أَن	ظَنَّ	إِنَّهُ
ya**h**oora	lan	an	**th**anna	Innahu
He would come back	Never	That	Thought	Verily He

إِنَّهُ ظَنَّ أَن لَّن يَحُورَ ۝

14. Innahu **th**anna an lan ya**h**oora

14 Verily, he thought that he would never come back (to Us)!

بَصِيرًا	بِهِ	كَانَ	رَبَّهُ	إِنَّ	بَلَى
ba**s**eer**a**n	bihi	k**a**na	rabbahu	inna	Bal**a**
Beholding	At him	Has been	His Lord	Verily	Yes

60

بَلَىٰ إِنَّ رَبَّهُۥ كَانَ بِهِۦ بَصِيرًا ۝

15. Bala inna rabbahu kana bihi baseeran

15 Yes! Verily, his Lord has been ever beholding him!

		بِالشَّفَقِ	أُقْسِمُ	فَلَا
		bialshshafaqi	oqsimu	Fala
		By the afterglow of sunset	I swear	So

فَلَآ أُقْسِمُ بِٱلشَّفَقِ ۝

16. Fala oqsimu bialshshafaqi

16 So I swear by the afterglow of sunset;

		وَسَقَ	وَمَا	وَٱللَّيْلِ
		Wasaqa	wama	Waallayli
		It gathers in its darkness	And whatever	And the night

وَٱلَّيْلِ وَمَا وَسَقَ ۝

17. Waallayli wama wasaqa

17 And by the night and whatever it gathers in its darkness;

		ٱتَّسَقَ	إِذَا	وَٱلْقَمَرِ
		Ittasaqa	itha	Waalqamari
		It is at the full	When	And the moon

وَٱلْقَمَرِ إِذَا ٱتَّسَقَ ۝

18. Waalqamari itha ittasaqa

18 And by the moon when it is at the full,

		طَبَقٍ	عَن	طَبَقًا	لَتَرْكَبُنَّ
		tabaqin	AAan	tabaqan	Latarkabunna
		Stage	From	To stage	You shall certainly travel

لَتَرْكَبُنَّ طَبَقًا عَن طَبَقٍ ﴿١٩﴾

19. Latarkabunna tabaqan AAan tabaqin

19 You shall certainly travel from stage to stage (in this life and in the Hereafter).

		يُؤْمِنُونَ	لَا	لَهُمْ	فَمَا
		yu/minoona	la	lahum	Fama
		They believe	Not	With them	What is the matter

فَمَا هُمْ لَا يُؤْمِنُونَ ﴿٢٠﴾

20. Fama lahum la yu/minoona

20 What is the matter with them, that they believe not?

يَسْجُدُونَ	لَا	الْقُرْآنُ	عَلَيْهِمُ	قُرِئَ	وَإِذَا
yasjudoona	la	alqur-anu	AAalayhimu	quri-a	Wa-itha
They fall prostrate	Not	The Quran	To them	Is recieted	And when

وَإِذَا قُرِئَ عَلَيْهِمُ ٱلْقُرْءَانُ لَا يَسْجُدُونَ ۩ ﴿٢١﴾

21. Wa-itha quri-a AAalayhimu alqur-anu la yasjudoona

21 And when the Qur'an is recited to them, they fall not prostrate, (Sada-e-Tilawath)

		يُكَذِّبُونَ	كَفَرُوا	الَّذِينَ	بَلِ
		yukaththiboona	kafaroo	allatheena	Bali
		Deny	Disbelieve	Those who	Nay

بَلِ ٱلَّذِينَ كَفَرُوا يُكَذِّبُونَ ﴿٢٢﴾

22. Bali allatheena kafaroo yukaththiboona

22 Nay, (on the contrary), those who disbelieve, belie (Prophet Muhammad ﷺ) and whatever he brought, i.e. this Qur'an and Islamic Monotheism, etc.).

		يُوعُونَ	بِمَا	أَعْلَمُ	وَاللَّهُ
		yooAAoona	bima	aAAlamu	WaAllahu
		They gather	What	Knows best	And Allah

وَٱللَّهُ أَعْلَمُ بِمَا يُوعُونَ ۝

23. WaAllahu aAAlamu bima yooAAoona

23 And Allah knows best what they gather (of good and bad deeds),

			أَلِيمٍ	بِعَذَابٍ	فَبَشِّرْهُم
			aleem**in**	biAAa**th**abin	Fabashshirhum
			Painful	A torment	So announce to them

فَبَشِّرْهُم بِعَذَابٍ أَلِيمٍ ۝

24. Fabashshirhum biAAa**th**abin aleem**in**

24 So announce to them a painful torment.

لَهُمْ	ٱلصَّالِحَاتِ	وَعَمِلُوا۟	آمَنُوا۟	ٱلَّذِينَ	إِلَّا
lahum	alssalihati	waAAamiloo	amanoo	alla**th**eena	Illa
For them	Righteous deeds	And do	Believe	Those who	Save

			مَمْنُونٍ	غَيْرُ	أَجْرٌ
			mamnoon**in**	ghayru	ajrun
			Ending	Never	(is) a reward

إِلَّا ٱلَّذِينَ ءَامَنُوا۟ وَعَمِلُوا۟ ٱلصَّٰلِحَٰتِ لَهُمْ أَجْرٌ غَيْرُ مَمْنُونٍ ۝

25. Illa alla**th**eena amanoo waAAamiloo alssalihati lahum ajrun ghayru mamnoon**in**

25 Save those who believe and do righteous good deeds, for them is a reward that will never come to an end (i.e. Paradise).

Surah # 85
AL-BURUJ

Makkia

سُورَةُ البُرُوجِ

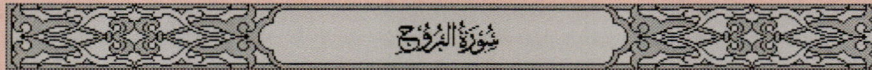

Verses 22
Sections 1

بِسْمِ اللهِ الرَّحْمٰنِ الرَّحِيمِ

			الْبُرُوجِ	ذَاتِ	وَالسَّمَاءِ
			alburooji	thati	Waalssama-i
			The big stars	With/holding	By the heavens

﷽ وَٱلسَّمَآءِ ذَاتِ ٱلْبُرُوجِ ۝

1. Waalssama-i thati alburooji
1 By the heaven, holding the big stars .

			الْمَوْعُودِ	وَالْيَوْمِ
			almawAAoodi	Waalyawmi
			Promised	And the day

وَٱلْيَوْمِ ٱلْمَوْعُودِ ۝

2. Waalyawmi almawAAoodi
2 And by the Promised Day (i.e. the Day of Resurrection);

			وَمَشْهُودٍ	وَشَاهِدٍ
			wamashhoodin	Washahidin
			And the witnessed day	And the witnessing day

وَشَاهِدٍ وَمَشْهُودٍ ۝

3. Washahidin wamashhoodin
3 And by the witnessing day (i.e. Friday), and by the witnessed day [i.e. the day of 'Arafat (*Hajj*) the ninth of Dhul-Hijjah];

		الْأُخْدُودِ	أَصْحَابُ	قُتِلَ
		alukhdoodi	as-habu	Qutila
		(of) th ditch	The people	Were cursed

قُتِلَ أَصْحَابُ ٱلْأُخْدُودِ ۝

4. Qutila as-habu alukhdoodi
4 Cursed were the people of the ditch (the story of the Boy and the King).

		الْوَقُودِ	ذَاتِ	النَّارِ
		alwaqoodi	thati	Alnnari

				Feul	With	(of) fire

الٓنَّارِ ذَاتِ ٱلۡوَقُودِ ۝

5. Alnnari thati alwaqoodi

5 Fire supplied (abundantly) with fuel,

		قُعُودٌ	عَلَيۡهَا	هُمۡ	إِذۡ
		quAAood**un**	AAalay**ha**	hum	I**th**
		Sat	By it	They	When

إِذۡ هُمۡ عَلَيۡهَا قُعُودٌ ۝

6. I**th** hum AAalay**ha** quAAood**un**

6 When they sat by it (fire),

شُهُودٌ	بِالۡمُؤۡمِنِينَ	يَفۡعَلُونَ	مَا	عَلَىٰ	وَهُمۡ
shuhood**un**	bi**a**lmu/minee**na**	yafAAaloona	m**a**	AAal**a**	Wahum
(were) witness	To the believers	They were doing	What	On	And they

وَهُمۡ عَلَىٰ مَا يَفۡعَلُونَ بِٱلۡمُؤۡمِنِينَ شُهُودٌ ۝

7. Wahum AAal**a** m**a** yafAAaloona bi**a**lmu/minee**na** shuhood**un**

7 And they witnessed what they were doing against the believers (i.e. burning them).

يُؤۡمِنُوا	أَن	إِلَّا	مِنۡهُمۡ	نَقَمُوا	وَمَا
yu/minoo	an	ill**a**	minhum	naqamoo	Wam**a**
They believed	That	Except	On them	They put revenge	And not

			الۡحَمِيدِ	الۡعَزِيزِ	بِاللَّهِ
			al**h**ameed**i**	alAAazeez**i**	bi**A**ll**a**hi
			Worthy of All praise	The Almighty	In Allah

وَمَا نَقَمُواْ مِنۡهُمۡ إِلَّآ أَن يُؤۡمِنُواْ بِٱللَّهِ ٱلۡعَزِيزِ ٱلۡحَمِيدِ ۝

8. Wam**a** naqamoo minhum ill**a** an yu/minoo bi**A**ll**a**hi alAAazeez**i** al**h**ameed**i**

8 They had nothing against them, except that they believed in Allah, the All-Mighty, Worthy of all Praise!

الَّذِي	لَهُ	مُلْكُ	السَّمَاوَاتِ	وَالْأَرْضِ	وَاللَّهُ
Allathee	lahu	mulku	alssamawati	waal-ardi	waAllahu
Who	To Him (belongs)	Dominion	(of) the Heavens	And the Earth	And Allah

عَلَى	كُلِّ	شَيْءٍ	شَهِيدٌ		
AAala	kulli	shay-in	shaheedun		
Over	Every	Thing	(is) witness		

ٱلَّذِى لَهُۥ مُلْكُ ٱلسَّمَـٰوَٰتِ وَٱلْأَرْضِ ۚ وَٱللَّهُ عَلَىٰ كُلِّ شَىْءٍ شَهِيدٌ ﴿٩﴾

9. Allathee lahu mulku alssamawati waal-ardi waAllahu AAala kulli shay-in shaheedun

9 Who, to Whom belongs the dominion of the heavens and the earth! And Allah is Witness over everything.

إِنَّ	الَّذِينَ	فَتَنُوا	الْمُؤْمِنِينَ	وَالْمُؤْمِنَاتِ	ثُمَّ
Inna	allatheena	fatanoo	almu/mineena	waalmu/minati	thumma
Verily	Those	Who put into trail	The believing men	And believing women	Then

لَمْ	يَتُوبُوا	فَلَهُمْ	عَذَابُ	جَهَنَّمَ	وَلَهُمْ
lam	yatooboo	falahum	AAathabu	jahannama	walahum
Not	They turn in repentance	Will have/ for them	Torment	(of) Hell	And they will have

		عَذَابُ	الْحَرِيقِ		
		AAathabu	alhareeqi		
		Punishment	(of) the burning fire		

إِنَّ ٱلَّذِينَ فَتَنُوا۟ ٱلْمُؤْمِنِينَ وَٱلْمُؤْمِنَـٰتِ ثُمَّ لَمْ يَتُوبُوا۟ فَلَهُمْ عَذَابُ جَهَنَّمَ وَلَهُمْ عَذَابُ ٱلْحَرِيقِ ﴿١٠﴾

10. Inna allatheena fatanoo almu/mineena waalmu/minati thumma lam yatooboo falahum AAathabu jahannama walahum AAathabu alhareeqi

10 Verily, those who put into trial the believing men and believing women (by torturing them and burning them), and then do not turn in repentance, (to Allah), will have the torment of Hell, and they will have the punishment of the burning Fire.

إِنَّ	الَّذِينَ	آمَنُوا	وَعَمِلُوا	الصَّالِحَاتِ	لَهُمْ
Inna	allatheena	amanoo	waAAamiloo	alssalihati	lahum

for them	The righteous deeds	And do	Believe	Those who	Verily
ذَلِكَ	الْأَنْهَارُ	تَحْتِهَا	مِن	تَجْرِي	جَنَّاتٌ
thalika	al-anharu	tahtiha	min	tajree	jannatun
That	Rivers	underneath		Flowing	(are) gardens
				الْكَبِيرُ	الْفَوْزُ
				alkabeeru	alfawzu
				Great	(is) the success

إِنَّ ٱلَّذِينَ ءَامَنُوا۟ وَعَمِلُوا۟ ٱلصَّٰلِحَٰتِ لَهُمْ جَنَّٰتٌ تَجْرِى مِن تَحْتِهَا ٱلْأَنْهَٰرُ ذَٰلِكَ ٱلْفَوْزُ ٱلْكَبِيرُ ﴿١١﴾

11. Inna allatheena amanoo waAAamiloo alssalihati lahum jannatun tajree min tahtiha al-anharu thalika alfawzu alkabeeru

11 Verily, those who believe and do righteous good deeds, for them will be Gardens under which rivers flow (Paradise). That is the great success.

		lashadeedun	rabbika	Batsha	Inna
		لَشَدِيدٌ	رَّبِّكَ	بَطْشَ	إِنَّ
		(is) indeed severe	(of) your Lord	Grip	Verily

إِنَّ بَطْشَ رَبِّكَ لَشَدِيدٌ ﴿١٢﴾

12. Inna batsha rabbika lashadeedun

12 Verily, (O Muhammad (ﷺ)) the Grip (Punishment) of your Lord is severe.

		wayuAAeedu	yubdi-o	huwa	Innahu
		وَيُعِيدُ	يُبْدِئُ	هُوَ	إِنَّهُ
		And repeats	Begins	(He)	Verily He (Allah)

إِنَّهُ هُوَ يُبْدِئُ وَيُعِيدُ ﴿١٣﴾

13. Innahu huwa yubdi-o wayuAAeedu

13 Verily, He it is Who begins (punishment) and repeats (punishment in the Hereafter) (or originates the creation of everything, and then repeats it on the Day of Resurrection).

			الْوَدُودُ	الْغَفُورُ	وَهُوَ
			alwadoodu	alghafooru	Wahuwa
			Full of Love	(is) Oft-Forgiving	And He

وَهُوَ ٱلْغَفُورُ ٱلْوَدُودُ ﴿١٤﴾

14. Wahuwa alghafooru alwadoodu

14 And He is Oft-Forgiving, full of love (towards the pious who are real true believers of Islamic Monotheism),

			الْمَجِيدُ	الْعَرْشِ	ذُو
			almajeedi	alAAarshi	Thoo
			The Glorious	(of) the Thorne	Owner

ذُو ٱلْعَرْشِ ٱلْمَجِيدُ ﴿١٥﴾

15. Thoo alAAarshi almajeedi

15 Owner of the throne, the Glorious

			يُرِيدُ	لِّمَا	فَعَّالٌ
			Yureedu	lima	FaAAAAalun
			He intends	Of what	He is the doer

فَعَّالٌ لِّمَا يُرِيدُ ﴿١٦﴾

16. FaAAAAalun lima yureedu

16 He does what He intends (or wills).

		الْجُنُودِ	حَدِيثُ	أَتَاكَ	هَلْ
		aljunoodi	hadeethu	ataka	Hal
		(of) the Hosts	The story	Reached you	Has

هَلْ أَتَىٰكَ حَدِيثُ ٱلْجُنُودِ ﴿١٧﴾

17. Hal ataka hadeethu aljunoodi

17 Has the story reached you of the hosts,

				وَثَمُودَ	فِرْعَوْنَ
				wathamooda	FirAAawna
				And Thamud	(of) pharaoh

فِرْعَوْنَ وَثَمُودَ ﴿١٨﴾

18. FirAAawna wathamooda

18 Of Fir'aun (Pharaoh) and Thamud?

تَكْذِيبٍ	فِي	كَفَرُوا	الَّذِينَ	بَلِ
taktheeb**in**	fee	kafaroo	allatheena	Bali
Denying	In	Desbeileve	Those who	Nay

بَلِ ٱلَّذِينَ كَفَرُوا۟ فِي تَكْذِيبٍ ﴿١٩﴾

19. Bali allatheena kafaroo fee taktheeb**in**

19 Nay! The disbelievers (persisted) in denying (Prophet Muhammad (ﷺ) and his Message of Islamic Monotheism).

	مُّحِيطٌ	وَرَائِهِم	مِن	وَٱللَّهُ
	muhee**t**un	wara-ihim	min	WaAllahu
	Encompasses	Behind them	From	And Allah

وَٱللَّهُ مِن وَرَآئِهِم مُّحِيطٌ ﴿٢٠﴾

20. WaAllahu min wara-ihim muhee**t**un

20 And Allah encompasses them from behind! (i.e. all their deeds are within His Knowledge, and He will requite them for their deeds).

	مَّجِيدٌ	قُرْآنٌ	هُوَ	بَلْ
	majeed**un**	qur-anun	huwa	Bal
	Glorious	(is) a Qur'an	This	Nay

بَلْ هُوَ قُرْءَانٌ مَّجِيدٌ ﴿٢١﴾

21. Bal huwa qur-anun majeed**un**

1 Nay! This is a Glorious Qur'an,

			مَّحْفُوظٍ	لَوْحٍ	فِي
			mahfoo_th_in	lawhin	Fee
			Preserved	Tablet	In

فِى لَوْحٍ مَّحْفُوظٍ ﴿٢٢﴾

22. Fee lawhin mahfoothin
22 (Inscribed) in *Al-Lauh Al-Mahfuz* (The Preserved Tablet)!

Surah # 86
AT-TARIQ
Makkia

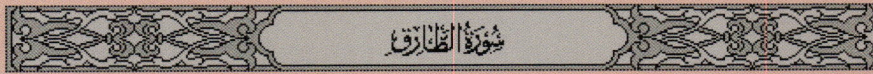

سُوْرَةُ الطَّارِقِ

Verses 17
Sections 1

بِسْمِ اللهِ الرَّحْمٰنِ الرَّحِيْمِ

				وَالطَّارِقِ	وَالسَّمَاء
				waalttariqi	Waalssama-i
				And At-Tariq (the night comer)	By the Heaven

﴿ وَٱلسَّمَآءِ وَٱلطَّارِقِ ١ ﴾

1. Waalssama-i waalttariqi
1 By the heaven, and At-Tariq (the night-comer, i.e. the bright star);

		الطَّارِقُ	مَا	أَدْرَاكَ	وَمَا
		alttariqu	ma	Adraka	Wama
		(is) At- Tariq (the night-comer)	What	Will make you know	And what

وَمَآ أَدْرَىٰكَ مَا ٱلطَّارِقُ ٢

2. Wama adraka ma alttariqu
2 And what will make you to know what *At-Tariq* (night-comer) is?

			النَّجْمُ الثَّاقِبُ	
			alththaqibu	Alnnajmu
			Piercing bright	(it is) the star

70

ٱلنَّجْمُ ٱلثَّاقِبُ ۞

3. Alnnajmu alththaqibu

3 (It is) the star of piercing brightness;

حَافِظٌ	عَلَيْهَا	لَّمَّا	نَفْسٍ	كُلُّ	إِن
hafi*th*un	AAalayha	lamma	nafsin	Kullu	In
(is) a protector	Over him	But	Human being	Every	(is) not

إِن كُلُّ نَفْسٍ لَّمَّا عَلَيْهَا حَافِظٌ ۞

4. In kullu nafsin lamma AAalayha hafi*th*un

4 There is no human being but has a protector over him (or her) (i.e. angels incharge of each human being guarding him, writing his good and bad deeds, etc.)

		خُلِقَ	مِمَّ	ٱلْإِنسَانُ	فَلْيَنظُرِ
		khuliqa	mimma	al-insanu	Falyan*th*uri
		He is created	From what	A man	So let see

فَلْيَنظُرِ ٱلْإِنسَانُ مِمَّ خُلِقَ ۞

5. Falyan*th*uri al-insanu mimma khuliqa

5 So let man see from what he is created!

		دَافِقٍ	مَّاءٍ	مِن	خُلِقَ
		Dafiq**in**	m**a**-in	min	Khuliq**a**
		Gushing forth	A water	From	He has created

خُلِقَ مِن مَّاءٍ دَافِقٍ ۞

6. Khuliqa min m**a**-in d**a**fiq**in**

6 He is created from a water gushing forth

وَٱلتَّرَائِب	ٱلصُّلْب	بَيْنِ	مِن	يَخْرُجُ
waalttara-ibi	alssulbi	bayni	min	Yakhruju
And the ribs	The back bone	Between	From	It proceeds

71

تَخْرُجُ مِنْ بَيْنِ ٱلصُّلْبِ وَٱلتَّرَآئِبِ ۝

7. Yakhruju min bayni alssulbi waalttara-ibi

7 Proceeding from between the back-bone and the ribs,

		لَقَادِرٌ	رَجْعِهِ	عَلَىٰ	إِنَّهُ
		laqadirun	rajAAihi	AAala	Innahu
		(is) able	Bring him back	To	Verily He (Allah)

إِنَّهُ عَلَىٰ رَجْعِهِ لَقَادِرٌ ۝

8. Innahu AAala rajAAihi laqadirun

8 Verily, (Allah) is Able to bring him back (to life)!

		ٱلسَّرَآئِرُ	تُبْلَى	يَوْمَ
		alssara-iru	tubla	Yawma
		The secrets	Will be examined	The day (when)

يَوْمَ تُبْلَى ٱلسَّرَآئِرُ ۝

9. Yawma tubla alssara-iru

9 The Day when all the secrets (deeds, prayers, fasting, etc.) will be examined (as to their truth).

نَاصِرٍ	وَلَا	قُوَّةٍ	مِن	لَهُ	فَمَا
nasirin	wala	quwwatin	min	lahu	Fama
Any helper	Nor	Power	Any	For him	Then not

فَمَا لَهُ مِن قُوَّةٍ وَلَا نَاصِرٍ ۝

10. Fama lahu min quwwatin wala nasirin

10 Then will (man) have no power, nor any helper.

		ٱلرَّجْعِ	ذَاتِ	وَٱلسَّمَآءِ
		alrrajAAi	thati	Waalssama-i
		The returning rain	With	By the sky

وَٱلسَّمَآءِ ذَاتِ ٱلرَّجْعِ ۞

11. Waalssama-i thati alrrajAAi

11 By the sky (having rain clouds) which gives rain, again and again.

			الصَّدْعِ	ذَاتِ	وَٱلْأَرْضِ
			alssadAAi	thati	Waal-ardi
			Split (It opens out for gushing of springs)	With	And the earth

وَٱلْأَرْضِ ذَاتِ ٱلصَّدْعِ ۞

12. Waal-ardi thati alssadAAi

12 And the earth which splits (with the growth of trees and plants),

			فَصْلٌ	لَقَوْلٌ	إِنَّهُ
			faslun	laqawlun	Innahu
			That separates	(is) the word	Verily this (Quran)

إِنَّهُ لَقَوْلٌ فَصْلٌ ۞

13. Innahu laqawlun faslun

13 Verily! This (the Qur'an) is the Word that separates (the truth from falsehood, and commands strict legal laws for mankind to cut the roots of evil).

			بِالْهَزْلِ	هُوَ	وَمَا
			bialhazli	huwa	Wama
			For amusement	It (is)	And not

وَمَا هُوَ بِٱلْهَزْلِ ۞

14. Wama huwa bialhazli

14 And it is not a thing for amusement.

			كَيْدًا	يَكِيدُونَ	إِنَّهُمْ
			kaydan	yakeedoona	Innahum
			A plot	Are plotting	Verily they

إِنَّهُمْ يَكِيدُونَ كَيْدًا ﴿١٥﴾

15. Innahum yakeedoona kaydan

15 Verily, they are but plotting a plot (against you O Muhammad 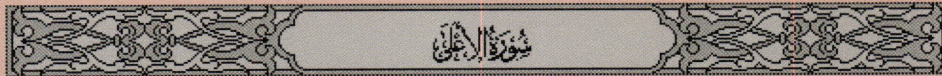).

				كَيْدًا	وَأَكِيدُ
				kaydan	Waakeedu
				A plan	And I am planning

وَأَكِيدُ كَيْدًا ﴿١٦﴾

16. Waakeedu kaydan
16 And I (too) am planning a plan.

رُوَيْدًا	أَمْهِلْهُمْ	الْكَافِرِينَ	فَمَهِّلِ
ruwaydan	amhilhum	Alkafireena	Famahhili
Gently (for a while)	Give respite to them	(to) the disbelievers	So give a respite

فَمَهِّلِ ٱلْكَفِرِينَ أَمْهِلْهُمْ رُوَيْدًا ﴿١٧﴾

17. Famahhili alkafireena amhilhum ruwaydan
17 So give a respite to the disbelievers. Deal you gently with them for a while.

Surah # 87
AL-ALA

Makkia

سورة الأعلى

Verses 19
Sections 1

بِسْمِ اللهِ الرَّحْمَنِ الرَّحِيمِ

	الْأَعْلَى	رَبِّكَ	اسْمَ	سَبِّحِ
	al-aAAla	rabbika	isma	Sabbihi

			The Most High	(of) your Lord	The name	Glorify

$$\text{﴿ سَبِّحِ ٱسْمَ رَبِّكَ ٱلْأَعْلَى ﴾}$$

1. Sabbihi isma rabbika al-aAAla
1 Glorify the Name of your Lord, the Most High,

			فَسَوَّى	خَلَقَ	الَّذِي
			fasawwa	khalaqa	Allathee
			And then proportioned	Created	Who

$$\text{ٱلَّذِى خَلَقَ فَسَوَّى ﴿٢﴾}$$

2. Allathee khalaqa fasawwa
2 Who has created (everything), and then proportioned it;

			فَهَدَى	قَدَّرَ	وَالَّذِي
			fahada	qaddara	Waallathee
			Then guided	Measured	And who

$$\text{وَٱلَّذِى قَدَّرَ فَهَدَى ﴿٣﴾}$$

3. Waallathee qaddara fahada
3 And Who has measured (preordainments for each and everything even to be blessed or wretched); then guided (i.e. showed mankind the right as well as wrong paths, and guided the animals to pasture);

			الْمَرْعَى	أَخْرَجَ	وَالَّذِي
			almarAAa	akhraja	Waallathee
			The pasturage	Brings out	And who

$$\text{وَٱلَّذِى أَخْرَجَ ٱلْمَرْعَى ﴿٤﴾}$$

4. Waallathee akhraja almarAAa
4 And Who brings out the pasturage,

			أَحْوَى	غُثَاء	فَجَعَلَهُ
			ahwa	ghuthaan	FajaAAalahu
			Dark	Stubble	And then makes it

فَجَعَلَهُۥ غُثَآءً أَحْوَىٰ ۝

5. FajaAAalahu ghuthaan ahwa

5 And then makes it dark stubble.

			تَنسَىٰ	فَلَا	سَنُقْرِئُكَ
			tansa	fala	Sanuqri-oka
			You shall forget	So not	We shall make you to reciete

سَنُقْرِئُكَ فَلَا تَنسَىٰ ۝

6. Sanuqri-oka fala tansa

6 We shall make you to recite (the Qur'an), so you (O Muhammad ﷺ) shall not forget (it),

يَعْلَمُ	إِنَّهُۥ	ٱللَّهُ	شَآءَ	مَا	إِلَّا
yaAAlamu	innahu	Allahu	Shaa	ma	Illa
Knows	Verily He (Allah)	Allah	Wills	What	Except

			يَخْفَىٰ	وَمَا	ٱلْجَهْرَ
			yakhfa	wama	aljahra
			Is hidden	And what	The apparent

إِلَّا مَا شَآءَ ٱللَّهُ ۚ إِنَّهُۥ يَعْلَمُ ٱلْجَهْرَ وَمَا يَخْفَىٰ ۝

7. Illa ma shaa Allahu innahu yaAAlamu aljahra wama yakhfa

7 Except what Allah, may will, He knows what is apparent and what is hidden.

			لِلْيُسْرَىٰ	وَنُيَسِّرُكَ
			lilyusra	Wanuyassiruka
			To the path	And we shall make easy for you

وَنُيَسِّرُكَ لِلْيُسْرَىٰ ۝

8. Wanuyassiruka lilyusra

8 And We shall make easy for you (O Muhammad ﷺ) the easy way (i.e. the doing of righteous deeds).

		الذِّكْرَى	نَّفَعَتِ	إِن	فَذَكِّرْ
		alththikra	nafaAAati	in	Fathakkir
		The admonition	Profits	If	Therefore give advice/admonition

فَذَكِّرْ إِن نَّفَعَتِ ٱلذِّكْرَىٰ ۝

9. Fathakkir in nafaAAati alththikra

9 Therefore remind (men) in case the reminder profits (them).

			يَخْشَى	مَن	سَيَذَّكَّرُ
			yakhsha	man	Sayaththakkaru
			Fears	Who	He will receive

سَيَذَّكَّرُ مَن يَخْشَىٰ ۝

10. Sayaththakkaru man yakhsha

10 The reminder will be received by him who fears (Allah),

				الْأَشْقَى	وَيَتَجَنَّبُهَا
				al-ashqa	Wayatajannabuha
				The wretched	And avoid it

وَيَتَجَنَّبُهَا ٱلْأَشْقَى ۝

11. Wayatajannabuha al-ashqa

11 But it will be avoided by the wretched,

		الْكُبْرَى	النَّارَ	يَصْلَى	الَّذِي
		alkubra	alnnara	yasla	Allathee
		Great	(in) the fire	Will burn	So who

ٱلَّذِى يَصْلَى ٱلنَّارَ ٱلْكُبْرَىٰ ۝

12. Allathee yasla alnnara alkubra

12 Who will enter the great Fire and made to taste its burning,

يَحْيَى	وَلَا	فِيهَا	يَمُوتُ	لَا	ثُمَّ
yahya	wala	feeha	yamootu	la	Thumma
live	Nor	In it	He will die	Neither	Then

ثُمَّ لَا يَمُوتُ فِيهَا وَلَا تَحْيَىٰ ۝

13. Thumma la yamootu feeha wala yahya

13 Wherein he will neither die (to be in rest) nor live (a good living).

		تَزَكَّى	مَن	أَفْلَحَ	قَدْ
		tazakka	man	aflaha	Qad
		Purifies himself	Whosoever	Shall achieve success	Indeed

قَدْ أَفْلَحَ مَن تَزَكَّىٰ ۝

14. Qad aflaha man tazakka

14 Indeed whosoever purifies himself (by avoiding polytheism and accepting Islamic Monotheism) shall achieve success,

		فَصَلَّى	رَبِّهِ	اسْمَ	وَذَكَرَ
		fasalla	rabbihi	isma	Wathakara
		And prays	(of) his Lord	The name	And remembers

وَذَكَرَ اسْمَ رَبِّهِ فَصَلَّى ۝

15. Wathakara isma rabbihi fasalla

15 And remembers (glorifies) the Name of his Lord (worships none but Allah), and prays (five compulsory prayers and *Nawafil additional prayers*).

		الدُّنْيَا	الْحَيَاةَ	تُؤْثِرُونَ	بَلْ
		alddunya	alhayata	tu/thiroona	Bal
		Worldly	The life	You prefer	Nay

بَلْ تُؤْثِرُونَ الْحَيَوٰةَ الدُّنْيَا ۝

16. Bal tu/thiroona alhayata alddunya

16 Nay, you prefer the life of this world;

			وَأَبْقَى	خَيْرٌ	وَالْآخِرَةُ
			waabqa	khayrun	Waal-akhiratu
			And more lasting	(is) better	Although the hereafter

وَٱلْأَخِرَةُ خَيْرٌ وَأَبْقَىٰ ﴿١٧﴾

17. Waal-akhiratu khayrun waabqa

17 Although the Hereafter is better and more lasting.

	الْأُولَى	الصُّحُفِ	لَفِي	هَذَا	إِنَّ
	al-oola	alssuhufi	lafee	hatha	Inna
	Former	The scriptures	(is) in	This	Verily

إِنَّ هَـٰذَا لَفِى ٱلصُّحُفِ ٱلْأُولَىٰ ﴿١٨﴾

18. Inna hatha lafee alssuhufi al-oola

18 Verily! This is in the former Scriptures,

			وَمُوسَى	إِبْرَاهِيمَ	صُحُفِ
			wamoosa	ibraheema	Suhufi
			And Musa (Moses)	(of) Ibrahim (Abraham)	The scriptures

صُحُفِ إِبْرَاهِيمَ وَمُوسَىٰ ﴿١٩﴾

19. Suhufi ibraheema wamoosa

19 The Scriptures of Ibrahim (Abraham) and Musa (Moses).

Surah # 88
AL-GHASHIYAH

ٱلْغَـٰشِيَةِ

Verses 26
Sections 1
Makkia

بِسْمِ اللهِ الرَّحْمٰنِ الرَّحِيمِ

		الْغَاشِيَةِ	حَدِيثُ	أَتَاكَ	هَلْ
		alghashiyati	hadeethu	ataka	Hal
		(of) the overwhelming	The narration	Come to you	Has

هَلْ أَتَىٰكَ حَدِيثُ ٱلْغَٰشِيَةِ ۝

1. Hal ataka hadeethu alghashiyati

1 Has there come to you the narration of the overwhelming (i.e. the Day of Resurrection);

			خَاشِعَةٌ	يَوْمَئِذٍ	وُجُوهٌ
			khashiAAatun	yawma-ithin	Wujoohun
			(will be) humiliated	That day	(Some) faces

وُجُوهٌ يَوْمَئِذٍ خَٰشِعَةٌ ۝

2. Wujoohun yawma-ithin khashiAAatun

2 Some faces, that Day, will be humiliated (in the Hell-fire, i.e. the faces of all disbelievers, Jews and Christians, etc.).

				نَّاصِبَةٌ	عَامِلَةٌ
				nasibatun	AAamilatun
				Weary	Labouring

عَامِلَةٌ نَّاصِبَةٌ ۝

3. AAamilatun nasibatun

3 Labouring (hard in the worldly life by worshipping others besides Allah), weary (in the Hereafter with humility and disgrace) .

			حَامِيَةً	نَارًا	تَصْلَىٰ
			hamiyatan	naran	Tasla
			Hot	In fire	They will burn/enter

تَصْلَىٰ نَارًا حَامِيَةً ۝

4. Tasla naran hamiyatan

4 They will enter in the hot blazing Fire,

آنِيَةٍ	عَيْنٍ	مِنْ	تُسْقَى
aniyatin	AAaynin	min	Tusqa
Boiling	A spring	From	They will be given to drink

تُسْقَى مِنْ عَيْنٍ ءَانِيَةٍ ۝

5. Tusqa min AAaynin aniyatin

5 They will be given to drink from a boiling spring,

ضَرِيعٍ	مِن	إِلَّا	طَعَامٌ	لَهُم	لَّيْسَ
dareeAAin	min	illa	taAAamun	lahum	Laysa
A poisonous thorny plant	From	But	Food	For them	(there will be no)

لَّيْسَ لَهُمْ طَعَامٌ إِلَّا مِن ضَرِيعٍ ۝

6. Laysa lahum taAAamun illa min dareeAAin

6 No food will there be for them but a poisonous thorny plant,

جُوعٍ	مِن	يُغْنِي	وَلَا	يُسْمِنُ	لَا
jooAAin	min	yughnee	wala	yusminu	La
Hunger	Against	Avail	Nor	That will nourish	Neither

لَّا يُسْمِنُ وَلَا يُغْنِي مِن جُوعٍ ۝

7. La yusminu wala yughnee min jooAAin

7 Which will neither nourish nor avail against hunger.

		نَّاعِمَةٌ	يَوْمَئِذٍ	وُجُوهٌ
		naAAimatun	yawma-ithin	Wujoohun
		(will be) joyful	That day	(other) faces

وُجُوهٌ يَوْمَئِذٍ نَّاعِمَةٌ ۝

8. Wujoohun yawma-ithin naAAimatun

8 (Other) faces, that Day, will be joyful,

				رَاضِيَةٌ	لِسَعْيِهَا
				radiyatun	LisaAAyiha
				Glad	With their endevour

لِسَعْيِهَا رَاضِيَةٌ ۝

9. LisaAAyiha radiyatun

9 Glad with their endeavour (for their good deeds which they did in this world, along with the true Faith of Islamic Monotheism).

			عَالِيَةٍ	جَنَّةٍ	فِي
			AAaliyatin	jannatin	Fee
			High	Garden (paradise)	In

فِي جَنَّةٍ عَالِيَةٍ ۝

10. Fee jannatin Aaaliyatin

10 In a lofty Paradise.

		لَاغِيَةً	فِيهَا	سْمَعُ	لَّا	ت
		laghiyatan	feeha	tasmaAAu	La	
		Vain talk	Therein	They shall hear	Neither	

لَّا تَسْمَعُ فِيهَا لَاغِيَةً ۝

11. La tasmaAAu feeha laghiyatan

11 Where they shall neither hear harmful speech nor falsehood,

			جَارِيَةٌ	عَيْنٌ	فِيهَا
			jariyatun	AAaynun	Feeha
			Running	A spring	Therein (will be)

فِيهَا عَيْنٌ جَارِيَةٌ ۝

12. Feeha AAaynun jariyatun

12 Therein will be a running spring,

			مَّرْفُوعَةٌ	سُرُرٌ	فِيهَا

				marfooAAatun	sururun	Feeha
				Raised high	Thrones	Therein (will be)

فِيهَا سُرُرٌ مَّرْفُوعَةٌ ۱۳

13. Feeha sururun marfooAAatun
13 Therein will be thrones raised high,

				mawdooAAatun	Waakwabun
				Set at hand	And cups

وَأَكْوَابٌ مَّوْضُوعَةٌ ۱٤

14. Waakwabun mawdooAAatun
14 And cups set at hand.

				Masfoofatun	Wanamariqu
				Set in rows	And cushions

وَنَمَارِقُ مَصْفُوفَةٌ ۱۵

15. Wanamariqu masfoofatun
15 And cushions set in rows,

				mabthoothatun	Wazarabiyyu
				Spread out	And rich carpets

وَزَرَابِيُّ مَبْثُوثَةٌ ۱٦

16. Wazarabiyyu mabthoothatun
16 And rich carpets (all) spread out.

خُلِقَتْ	كَيْفَ	الْإِبِلِ	إِلَى	يَنظُرُونَ	أَفَلَا
khuliqat	kayfa	al-ibili	ila	yanthuroona	Afala
They are created	How	The camels	At	They look	Do not

أَفَلَا يَنظُرُونَ إِلَى ٱلْإِبِلِ كَيْفَ خُلِقَتْ ﴿١٧﴾

17. Afala yanthuroona ila al-ibili kayfa khuliqat

17 Do they not look at the camels, how they are created?

		رُفِعَتْ	كَيْفَ	السَّمَاء	وَإِلَى
		rufiAAat	kayfa	alssama-i	Wa-ila
		It is raised	How	The heavens	And at

وَإِلَى ٱلسَّمَاءِ كَيْفَ رُفِعَتْ ﴿١٨﴾

18. Wa-ila alssama-i kayfa rufiAAat

18 And at the heaven, how it is raised?

		نُصِبَتْ	كَيْفَ	الْجِبَالِ	وَإِلَى
		Nusibat	kayfa	aljibali	Wa-ila
		They are rooted and fixed firm	How	mountains	And at

وَإِلَى ٱلْجِبَالِ كَيْفَ نُصِبَتْ ﴿١٩﴾

19. Wa-ila aljibali kayfa nusibat

19 And at the mountains, how they are rooted and fixed firm?

		سُطِحَتْ	كَيْفَ	الْأَرْضِ	وَإِلَى
		Sutihat	kayfa	al-ardi	Wa-ila
		It is spread out	how	The earth	And at

وَإِلَى ٱلْأَرْضِ كَيْفَ سُطِحَتْ ﴿٢٠﴾

20. Wa-ila al-ardi kayfa sutihat

20 And at the earth, how it is spread out?

		مُذَكِّرٌ	أَنتَ	إِنَّمَا	فَذَكِّرْ
		Muthakkirun	anta	innama	Fathakkir

		Are a remainder	You	Only	So remember

فَذَكِّرْ إِنَّمَآ أَنتَ مُذَكِّرٌ ۝

21. Fathakkir innama anta muthakkirun

21 So remind them (O Muhammad (ﷺ)), you are only a one who reminds.

		بِمُصَيْطِرٍ	عَلَيْهِم	لَّسْتَ
		bimusaytirin	AAalayhim	Lasta
		A dictator	Over them	You are not

لَّسْتَ عَلَيْهِم بِمُصَيْطِرٍ ۝

22. Lasta AAalayhim bimusaytirin

22 You are not a dictator over them.

	وَكَفَرَ	تَوَلَّىٰ	مَن	إِلَّا
	wakafara	tawalla	man	Illa
	And disbelievers	Turns away	The one who	Save

إِلَّا مَن تَوَلَّىٰ وَكَفَرَ ۝

23. Illa man tawalla wakafara

23 Save the one who turns away and disbelieves

	الْأَكْبَرَ	الْعَذَابَ	اللَّهُ	فَيُعَذِّبُهُ
	al-akbara	alAAathaba	Allahu	FayuAAaththibuhu
	Greatest	The punishment	Allah	Then will punish him

فَيُعَذِّبُهُ اللَّهُ الْعَذَابَ الْأَكْبَرَ ۝

24. FayuAAaththibuhu Allahu alAAathaba al-akbara

24 Then Allah will punish him with the greatest punishment.

		إِيَابَهُمْ	إِلَيْنَا	إِنَّ
		iyabahum	ilayna	Inna
		(will be) their return	To us	Verily

إِنَّ إِلَيْنَآ إِيَابَهُمْ ۝

25. Inna ilayna iyabahum
25 Verily, to Us will be their return;

ثُمَّ إِنَّ عَلَيْنَا حِسَابَهُمْ

		hisabahum	AAalayna	inna	Thumma
		(will be) their return	For Us	Verily	Then

ثُمَّ إِنَّ عَلَيْنَا حِسَابَهُم ۝

26. Thumma inna AAalayna hisabahum
26 Then verily, for Us will be their reckoning.

Surah # 89
AL-FAJR
Makkia

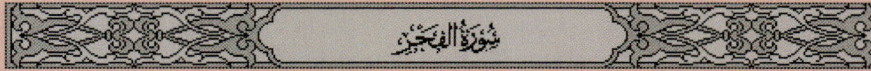

Verses 30
Sections 1

بِسْمِ اللهِ الرَّحْمٰنِ الرَّحِيمِ

وَالْفَجْرِ

					Waalfajri
					By the dawn

وَالْفَجْرِ ۝

1. Waalfajri
1 By the dawn;

وَلَيَالٍ عَشْرٍ

				AAashrin	Walayalin
				Ten	And by the nights

$$\text{وَلَيَالٍ عَشْرٍ} \; ﴿٢﴾$$

2. Walayalin AAashr**in**

2 By the ten nights (i.e. the first ten days of the month of Dhul-Hijjah),

				وَالْوَتْرِ	وَالشَّفْعِ
				waalwatri	WaalshshafAAi
				And by the odd	And by the even

$$\text{وَالشَّفْعِ وَالْوَتْرِ} \; ﴿٣﴾$$

3. WaalshshafAAi waalwat**ri**

3 And by the even and the odd (of all the creations of Allah).

			يَسْرِ	إِذَا	وَاللَّيْلِ
			yasri	itha	Waallayli
			It departs	When	And by the night

$$\text{وَاللَّيْلِ إِذَا يَسْرِ} \; ﴿٤﴾$$

4. Waallayli i_tha yas**ri**

4 And by the night when it departs

حِجْرٍ	لِّذِي	قَسَمٌ	ذَلِكَ	فِي	هَلْ
hijr**in**	lithee	qasamun	thalika	fee	Hal
(of) understanding	For those (men)	An oath / evidence	Them	In	Is it

$$\text{هَلْ فِي ذَلِكَ قَسَمٌ لِّذِي حِجْرٍ} \; ﴿٥﴾$$

5. Hal fee _thalika qasamun lithee hijr**in**

5 There is indeed in them (the above oaths) sufficient proofs for men of understanding (and that, they should avoid all kinds of sins and disbeliefs, etc.)!

بِعَادٍ	رَبُّكَ	فَعَلَ	كَيْفَ	تَرَ	أَلَمْ
biAAad**in**	rabbuka	faAAala	kayfa	tara	Alam
With Ad	Your lord	Dealt	How	You see	Did not

أَلَمْ تَرَ كَيْفَ فَعَلَ رَبُّكَ بِعَادٍ ۝

6. Alam tara kayfa faAAala rabbuka biAAadin

6 Did you (O Muhammad (ﷺ)) not see (thought) how your Lord dealt with 'Ad (people)?

			الْعِمَادِ	ذَاتِ	إِرَمَ
			alAAimadi	thati	Irama
			Pillars	Of	(of) Iram

إِرَمَ ذَاتِ ٱلْعِمَادِ ۝

7. Irama thati alAAimadi

7 Who were very tall like lofty pillars,

الْبِلَادِ	فِي	مِثْلُهَا	يُخْلَقْ	لَمْ	الَّتِي
albiladi	fee	mithluha	yukhlaq	lam	Allatee
The Land	In	Like them	Were created	Not	Which

ٱلَّتِي لَمْ تُخْلَقْ مِثْلُهَا فِي ٱلْبِلَدِ ۝

8. Allatee lam yukhlaq mithluha fee albiladi

8 The like of which were not created in the land?

بِالْوَادِ	الصَّخْرَ	جَابُوا	الَّذِينَ	وَثَمُودَ
bialwadi	alssakhra	jaboo	allatheena	Wathamooda
In a vlley	Rocks	Hewed/cut out	Who	And (with) thamud

وَثَمُودَ ٱلَّذِينَ جَابُوا ٱلصَّخْرَ بِٱلْوَادِ ۝

9. Wathamooda allatheena jaboo alssakhra bialwadi

9 And (with) Thamud (people), who cut (hewed) out rocks in the valley (to make dwellings)?

			الْأَوْتَادِ	ذِي	وَفِرْعَوْنَ
			al-awtadi	thee	WafirAAawna
			the stakes	With	And (with) pharoh

وَفِرْعَوْنَ ذِى ٱلْأَوْتَادِ ۝

10. WafirAAawna thee al-awtadi

10 And (with) Fir'aun (Pharaoh), who had pegs (who used to torture men by binding them to pegs)?

الْبَلَادِ	فِي	طَغَوْا	الَّذِينَ
albiladi	fee	taghaw	Allatheena
The lands	In	Transgressed beyond bounds	Who

ٱلَّذِينَ طَغَوْا۟ فِى ٱلْبِلَٰدِ ۝

11. Allatheena taghaw fee albiladi

11 Who did transgress beyond bounds in the lands (in the disobedience of Allah).

		الْفَسَادَ	فِيهَا	فَأَكْثَرُوا
		alfasada	feeha	Faaktharoo
		Mischief	Therein	And made much

فَأَكْثَرُوا۟ فِيهَا ٱلْفَسَادَ ۝

12. Faaktharoo feeha alfasada

12 And made therein much mischief.

عَذَاب	سَوْطَ	رَبُّكَ	عَلَيْهِمْ	فَصَبَّ
AAathabin	sawta	rabbuka	AAalayhim	Fasabba
(of) torment	Lash , whp	Your Lord	On them	So poured

فَصَبَّ عَلَيْهِمْ رَبُّكَ سَوْطَ عَذَابٍ ۝

13. Fasabba AAalayhim rabbuka sawta AAathabin

13 So your Lord poured on them different kinds of severe torment.

		لَبِالْمِرْصَادِ	رَبَّكَ	إِنَّ
		labialmirsadi	rabbaka	Inna
		(is) ever watchful	Your Lord	Verily

إِنَّ رَبَّكَ لَبِالْمِرْصَادِ ﴿١٤﴾

14. Inna rabbaka labi**almirsa**d**i**

14 Verily, your Lord is Ever Watchful (over them).

فَأَمَّا	الْإِنسَانُ	إِذَا	مَا	ابْتَلَاهُ	رَبُّهُ
Faamma	al-insanu	itha	ma	ibtalahu	rabbuhu
As for	A man	When		Tries him	His Lord

فَأَكْرَمَهُ	وَنَعَّمَهُ	فَيَقُولُ	رَبِّي	أَكْرَمَنِ
faakramahu	wanaAAAAamahu	fayaqoolu	rabbee	akramani
And gives him honour	And gives him bounties	He says	My Lord	Has honoured me

فَأَمَّا الْإِنسَـٰنُ إِذَا مَا ابْتَلَىٰهُ رَبُّهُۥ فَأَكْرَمَهُۥ وَنَعَّمَهُۥ فَيَقُولُ رَبِّىٓ أَكْرَمَنِ ﴿١٥﴾

15. Faamma al-insanu itha ma ibtalahu rabbuhu faakramahu wanaAAAAamahu fayaqoolu rabbee akramani

15 As for man, when his Lord tries him by giving him honour and gifts, then he says (puffed up): "My Lord has honoured me."

وَأَمَّا	إِذَا	مَا	ابْتَلَاهُ	فَقَدَرَ	عَلَيْهِ
Waamma	itha	ma	Ibtalahu	faqadara	AAalayhi
But	When		He tries him	straitening	Upon him

رِزْقَهُ	فَيَقُولُ	رَبِّي	أَهَانَنِ		
rizqahu	fayaqoolu	rabbee	ahanani		
His means of life	Then He says	My Lord	Has humiliated me		

وَأَمَّآ إِذَا مَا ابْتَلَىٰهُ فَقَدَرَ عَلَيْهِ رِزْقَهُۥ فَيَقُولُ رَبِّىٓ أَهَـٰنَنِ ﴿١٦﴾

16. Waamma itha ma ibtalahu faqadara AAalayhi rizqahu fayaqoolu rabbee ahanani

16 But when He tries him, by straitening his means of life, he says: "My Lord has humiliated me!"

كَلَّا	بَل	لَّا	تُكْرِمُونَ	الْيَتِيمَ

alyateema	tukrimoona	la	bal	Kalla
The orphans	You treat with generousity	Not	But	Nay

$$كَلَّا بَل لَّا تُكْرِمُونَ ٱلْيَتِيمَ ۝$$

17. Kalla bal la tukrimoona alyateema

17 Nay! But you treat not the orphans with kindness and generosity (i.e. you neither treat them well, nor give them their exact right of inheritance)!

المِسْكِين	طَعَامِ	عَلَى	تَحَاضُّونَ	وَلَا
almiskeeni	taAAami	AAala	tahaddoona	Wala
(of) the poor	Feeding	On	You urge one another	And not

$$وَلَا تَحَٰضُّونَ عَلَىٰ طَعَامِ ٱلْمِسْكِينِ ۝$$

18. Wala tahaddoona AAala taAAami almiskeeni

18 And urge not on the feeding of *AlMiskin* (the poor)!

		لَّمًّا	أَكْلًا	ٱلتُّرَاثَ	وَتَأْكُلُونَ
		lamman	aklan	altturatha	Wata/kuloona
		(with) greed	Devouring	The inheritance	And you devour

$$وَتَأْكُلُونَ ٱلتُّرَاثَ أَكْلًا لَّمًّا ۝$$

19. Wata/kuloona altturatha aklan lamman

19 And you devour inheritance all with greed,

		جَمًّا	حُبًّا	ٱلْمَالَ	وَتُحِبُّونَ
		jamman	hubban	almala	Watuhibboona
		Much	With love	Wealth	And you love

$$وَتُحِبُّونَ ٱلْمَالَ حُبًّا جَمًّا ۝$$

20. Watuhibboona almala hubban jamman

20 And you love wealth with much love!

دَكًّا	دَكًّا	ٱلْأَرْضُ	دُكَّتِ	إِذَا	كَلَّا
dakkan	dakkan	al-ardu	dukkati	itha	Kalla

Any	When	Is ground	The earth	With exceeding grinding

$$\text{كَلَّا إِذَا دُكَّتِ الْأَرْضُ دَكًّا دَكًّا} \quad ٢١$$

21. Kalla itha dukkati al-ardu dakkan dakkan

21 Nay! When the earth is ground to powder,

And comes	Your Lord	With the angels		
Wajaa	rabbuka	waalmalaku	saffan	Saffan
		In rows	saffan	Saffan

$$\text{وَجَاءَ رَبُّكَ وَالْمَلَكُ صَفًّا صَفًّا} \quad ٢٢$$

22. Wajaa rabbuka waalmalaku saffan saffan

22 And your Lord comes with the angels in rows,

And will be brought near	That day	Hell	On that day	Will remember	Man
Wajee-a	yawma-ithin	bijahannama	yawma-ithin	yatathakkaru	al-insanu

But how	(will avail) him	The remembrance			
waanna	lahu	alththikra			

$$\text{وَجِايءَ يَوْمَئِذٍ بِجَهَنَّمَ يَوْمَئِذٍ يَتَذَكَّرُ الْإِنسَانُ وَأَنَّى لَهُ الذِّكْرَى} \quad ٢٣$$

23. Wajee-a yawma-ithin bijahannama yawma-ithin yatathakkaru al-insanu waanna lahu alththikra

23 And Hell will be brought near that Day. On that Day will man remember, but how will that remembrance (then) avail him?

He will say	Would that I	Had sent forth	For my life
Yaqoolu	ya	laytanee	qaddamtu	lihayatee

$$\text{يَقُولُ يَا لَيْتَنِي قَدَّمْتُ لِحَيَاتِي} \quad ٢٤$$

24. Yaqoolu ya laytanee qaddamtu lihayatee

24 He will say: "Alas! Would that I had sent forth (good deeds) for (this) my life!"

أَحَدٌ	عَذَابَهُ	يُعَذِّبُ	لَّا	فَيَوْمَئِذٍ
ahad**un**	AAa<u>th</u>abahu	yuAAa<u>ththibu</u>	<u>la</u>	Fayawma-i<u>th</u>in
Anyone	(like) his punishment	Will punish	None	So on that day

فَيَوْمَئِذٍ لَّا يُعَذِّبُ عَذَابَهُ أَحَدٌ ۝

25. Fayawma-i<u>th</u>in <u>la</u> yuAAa<u>ththibu</u> AAa<u>th</u>abahu ahadun

25 So on that Day, none will punish as He will punish.

	أَحَدٌ	وَثَاقَهُ	يُوثِقُ	وَلَا
	ahad**un**	wa<u>th</u>aqahu	yoo<u>th</u>iqu	Wa<u>la</u>
	anyone	(like) His Binding	Will bind	And none

وَلَا يُوثِقُ وَثَاقَهُ أَحَدٌ ۝

26. Wa<u>la</u> yoo<u>th</u>iqu wa<u>th</u>aqahu ahadun

26 And none will bind as He will bind.

		الْمُطْمَئِنَّةُ	النَّفْسُ	أَيَّتُهَا	يَا
		almu<u>t</u>ma-inna**tu**	alnnafsu	ayyatuha	Ya
		In satisfaction	The soul	you	O

يَا أَيَّتُهَا النَّفْسُ الْمُطْمَئِنَّةُ ۝

27. Ya ayyatuha alnnafsu almu<u>t</u>ma-innatu****

27 (It will be said to the pious): "O (you) the one in (complete) rest and satisfaction!

مَّرْضِيَّةً	رَاضِيَةً	رَبِّكِ	إِلَى	ارْجِعِي
mardiyyatan	radiyatan	Rabbiki	ila	IrjiAAee
And well-pleasing (unto) Him	Well pleased (yourself)	Your Lord	To	Come back

ارْجِعِي إِلَى رَبِّكِ رَاضِيَةً مَّرْضِيَّةً ۝

28. IrjiAAee ila rabbiki radiyatan mardiyyatan

28 "Come back to your Lord, Well-pleased (yourself) and well-pleasing unto Him!

			AAibadee	fee	Faodkhulee
			My slaves	Among	Enter you then

عِبَادِي | فِي | فَادْخُلِي

فَادْخُلِي فِي عِبَادِي ﴿٢٩﴾

29. Faodkhulee fee AAibadee
29 "Enter you, then, among My honoured slaves,

			jannatee		Waodkhulee
			M		And enter you
			My Paradise		

جَنَّتِي | وَادْخُلِي

وَادْخُلِي جَنَّتِي ﴿٣٠﴾

30. Waodkhulee jannatee
30 "And enter you My Paradise!"

Surah # 90
AL-BALAD

Makkia

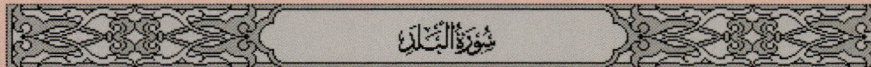

Verses 20
Sections 1

بِسْمِ اللَّهِ الرَّحْمَنِ الرَّحِيمِ

		albaladi	bihatha	oqsimu	La
		City (makkah)	By this		I swear

الْبَلَدِ | بِهَذَا | أُقْسِمُ | لَا

لَا أُقْسِمُ بِهَذَا الْبَلَدِ ﴿١﴾

1. La oqsimu bihatha albaladi
1 I swear by this city (Makkah);

94

		البَلَدِ	بِهَٰذَا	حِلٌّ	وَأَنتَ
		albaladi	bihatha	hillun	Waanta
		City	In this	(are) free (from) sin	And you

$$وَأَنتَ حِلٌّ بِهَٰذَا ٱلْبَلَدِ ۝$$

2. Waanta hillun bihatha albaladi

And you are free (from sin, to punish the enemies of Islam on the Day of the conquest) in this city (Makkah),

		وَلَدَ	وَمَا	وَوَالِدٍ
		walada	wama	Wawalidin
		He begot	At that which	And by the begetter

$$وَوَالِدٍ وَمَا وَلَدَ ۝$$

3. Wawalidin wama walada

3 And by the begetter (i.e. Adam) and that which he begot (i.e. his progeny);

كَبَدٍ	فِي	الْإِنسَانَ	خَلَقْنَا	لَقَدْ
kabadin	fee	al-insana	khalaqna	Laqad
Toil	In	Man	We have created	Verily

$$لَقَدْ خَلَقْنَا ٱلْإِنسَٰنَ فِي كَبَدٍ ۝$$

4. Laqad khalaqna al-insana fee kabadin

4 Verily, We have created man in toil.

أَحَدٌ	عَلَيْهِ	يَقْدِرَ	لَّن	أَن	أَيَحْسَبُ
ahadun	AAalayhi	yaqdira	lan	an	Ayahsabu
anyone	Him	Can overcome	Not	That	Does he think

$$أَيَحْسَبُ أَن لَّن يَقْدِرَ عَلَيْهِ أَحَدٌ ۝$$

5. Ayahsabu an lan yaqdira AAalayhi ahadun

5 Thinks he that none can overcome him?

		lubadan	malan	ahlaktu	Yaqoolu
		In abundance	Wealth	I have wasted	He says

لُّبَدًا   مَالًا   أَهْلَكْتُ   يَقُولُ

يَقُولُ أَهْلَكْتُ مَالًا لُّبَدًا ﴿٦﴾

6. Yaqoolu ahlaktu malan lubadan

6 He says (boastfully): "I have wasted wealth in abundance!"

	ahadun	Yarahu	lam	an	Ayahsabu
	Anyone	Sees him	Not	That	Does he think

أَحَدٌ   يَرَهُ   لَّمْ   أَن   أَيَحْسَبُ

أَيَحْسَبُ أَن لَّمْ يَرَهُ أَحَدٌ ﴿٧﴾

7. Ayahsabu an lam yarahu ahadun

7 Thinks he that none sees him?

	AAaynayni	lahu	najAAal	Alam
	A pair of eyes	For him	We made	Have not

عَيْنَيْنِ   لَّهُ   نَجْعَل   أَلَمْ

أَلَمْ نَجْعَل لَّهُ عَيْنَيْنِ ﴿٨﴾

8. Alam najAAal lahu AAaynayni

8 Have We not made for him a pair of eyes?

			washafatayni	Walisanan
			And a pair of lips	And a tongue

وَشَفَتَيْنِ   وَلِسَانًا

وَلِسَانًا وَشَفَتَيْنِ ﴿٩﴾

9. Walisanan washafatayni

9 And a tongue and a pair of lips?

			alnnajdayni	Wahadaynahu
			The two ways	And shown him

النَّجْدَيْنِ   وَهَدَيْنَاهُ

وَهَدَيْنَهُ ٱلنَّجْدَيْنِ ﴿١٠﴾

10. Wahadaynahu alnnajdayni

10 And shown him the two ways (good and evil)?

			الْعَقَبَةَ	اقْتَحَمَ	فَلَا
			alAAaqabata	iqtahama	Fala
			The steep path	He has attempted to pass on	But not

فَلَا ٱقْتَحَمَ ٱلْعَقَبَةَ ﴿١١﴾

11. Fala iqtahama alAAaqabata

11 But he has made no effort to pass on the path that is steep.

		الْعَقَبَةُ	مَا	أَدْرَاكَ	وَمَا
		alAAaqabatu	ma	adraka	Wama
		(is) the steep step	What	Will make you know	And what

وَمَا أَدْرَىٰكَ مَا ٱلْعَقَبَةُ ﴿١٢﴾

12. Wama adraka ma alAAaqabatu

12 And what will make you know the path that is steep?

				رَقَبَةٍ	فَكُّ
				raqabatin	Fakku
				A neck	(it is) freeing

فَكُّ رَقَبَةٍ ﴿١٣﴾

13. Fakku raqabatin

13 (It is) Freeing a neck (slave, etc.)

مَسْغَبَةٍ	ذِي	يَوْمٍ	فِي	إِطْعَامٌ	أَوْ
masghabatin	thee	yawmin	fee	itAAamun	Aw
hunger	with	A day	In	Giving food	Or

$$\text{أَوْ إِطْعَامٌ فِي يَوْمٍ ذِي مَسْغَبَةٍ ﴿١٤﴾}$$

14. Aw itAAamun fee yawmin thee masghabatin
14 Or giving food in a day of hunger (famine),

			مَقْرَبَةٍ	ذَا	يَتِيمًا
			maqrabatin	tha	Yateeman
			Near of kin		(to) an orphan

$$\text{يَتِيمًا ذَا مَقْرَبَةٍ ﴿١٥﴾}$$

15. Yateeman tha maqrabatin
15 To an orphan near of kin.

			مَتْرَبَةٍ	ذَا	مِسْكِينًا	أَوْ
			matrabatin	tha	miskeenan	Aw
			Afflicted with misery		(to) a poor	Or

$$\text{أَوْ مِسْكِينًا ذَا مَتْرَبَةٍ ﴿١٦﴾}$$

16. Aw miskeenan tha matrabatin
16 Or to a *Miskin* (poor) afflicted with misery.

وَتَوَاصَوْا	آمَنُوا	الَّذِينَ	مِنَ	كَانَ	ثُمَّ
watawasaw	amanoo	allatheena	mina	kana	Thumma
And recommended one another	Believed	Those who	(one) of	He became	Then

			بِالْمَرْحَمَةِ	وَتَوَاصَوْا	بِالصَّبْرِ
			bialmarhamati	watawasaw	bialssabri
			To pity	And tecomended one another	To the patience

$$\text{ثُمَّ كَانَ مِنَ الَّذِينَ ءَامَنُوا وَتَوَاصَوْا بِالصَّبْرِ وَتَوَاصَوْا بِالْمَرْحَمَةِ ﴿١٧﴾}$$

17. Thumma kana mina allatheena amanoo watawasaw bialssabri watawasaw bialmarhamati
17 Then he became one of those who believed, and recommended one another to perseverance and patience, and (also) recommended one another to pity and compassion.

			almaymanati	as-habu	Ola-ika
			(of) the right hand	(are) the companions	They

أُوْلَٰئِكَ أَصْحَٰبُ ٱلْمَيْمَنَةِ ﴿١٨﴾

18. Ola-ika as-habu almaymanati

18 They are those on the Right Hand (the dwellers of Paradise),

almash-amati	as-habu	hum	bi-ayatina	kafaroo	Waallatheena
(of) the left hand	(are) the companions	They	In Our signs/ verses	Disbelieved	But those who

وَٱلَّذِينَ كَفَرُوا۟ بِـَٔايَٰتِنَا هُمْ أَصْحَٰبُ ٱلْمَشْـَٔمَةِ ﴿١٩﴾

19. Waallatheena kafaroo bi-ayatina hum as-habu almash-amati

19 But those who disbelieved in Our *Ayat* (proofs, evidences, verses, lessons, signs, revelations, etc.), they are those on the Left Hand (the dwellers of Hell).

		mu/sadatun	narun	AAalayhim
		(will be) shut	The fire	Over them

عَلَيْهِمْ نَارٌ مُّؤْصَدَةٌ ﴿٢٠﴾

20. AAalayhim narun mu/sadatun

20 The Fire will be shut over them (i.e. they will be enveloped by the Fire without any opening or window or outlet.

Surah # 91
ASH-SHAMS

Makkia

سُورَةُ الشَّمْسِ

Verses 15
Sections 1

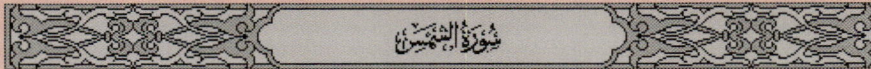

				وَضُحَاهَا	وَالشَّمْسِ
				waduhaha	Waalshshamsi
				And its brightness	By sun

وَالشَّمْسِ وَضُحَٰهَا ۝

1. Waalshshamsi waduhaha
1 And by the sun and its brightness;

			تَلَاهَا	إِذَا	وَالْقَمَرِ
			talaha	itha	Waalqamari
			It follows it	As / when	By the moon

وَالْقَمَرِ إِذَا تَلَٰهَا ۝

2. Waalqamari itha talaha
2 And by the moon as it follows it (the sun);

			جَلَّاهَا	إِذَا	وَالنَّهَارِ
			jallaha	itha	Waalnnahari
			It shows up (sun's Brightness)	As/when	And by day

وَالنَّهَارِ إِذَا جَلَّٰهَا ۝

3. Waalnnahari itha jallaha
3 And by the day as it shows up (the sun's) brightness;

			يَغْشَاهَا	إِذَا	وَاللَّيْلِ
			yaghshaha	itha	Waallayli
			It conceals it	As/when	By the night

وَالَّيْلِ إِذَا يَغْشَٰهَا ۝

4. Waallayli itha yaghshaha
4 And by the night as it conceals it (the sun);

			بَنَاهَا	وَمَا	وَالسَّمَاء

			Banaha	wama	Waalssama-i
			Who built it	And Him	By the heaven

وَٱلسَّمَآءِ وَمَا بَنَـٰهَا ۞

5. Waalssama-i wama banaha

5 And by the heaven and Him Who built it;

			tahaha	wama	Waal-ardi
			Who spread it	And Him	By the Earth

وَٱلْأَرْضِ وَمَا طَحَـٰهَا ۞

6. Waal-ardi wama tahaha

6 And by the earth and Him Who spread it,

			sawwaha	wama	Wanafsin
			Who perfected him in proportion	And Him	And by the Persons (soul)

وَنَفْسٍ وَمَا سَوَّىٰهَا ۞

7. Wanafsin wama sawwaha

7 And by *Nafs* (Adam or a person or a soul, etc.), and Him Who perfected him in proportion;

			wataqwaha	fujooraha	Faalhamaha
			And its purity, right	Its impurity, wrong	Then He (showed)

فَأَلْهَمَهَا فُجُورَهَا وَتَقْوَىٰهَا ۞

8. Faalhamaha fujooraha wataqwaha

8 Then He showed him what is wrong for him and what is right for him;

		zakkaha	man	aflaha	Qad
		Purifies his ownself	Who	He succeeds	Indeed

قَدْ أَفْلَحَ مَن زَكَّىٰهَا ﴿٩﴾

9. Qad aflaha man zakkaha

9 Indeed he succeeds who purifies his ownself (i.e. obeys and performs all that Allah ordered, by following the true Faith of Islamic Monotheism and by doing righteous good deeds).

		دَسَّاهَا	مَن	خَابَ	وَقَدْ
		Dassaha	man	khaba	Waqad
		Corrupts his ownself	Who	He fails	And indeed

وَقَدْ خَابَ مَن دَسَّىٰهَا ﴿١٠﴾

10. Waqad khaba man dassaha

10 And indeed he fails who corrupts his ownself (i.e. disobeys what Allah has ordered by rejecting the true Faith of Islamic Monotheism or by following polytheism, etc. or by doing every kind of evil wicked deeds).

		بِطَغْوَاهَا	ثَمُودُ	كَذَّبَتْ
		bitaghwaha	thamoodu	Kaththabat
		Through their transgression	Thamud	Denied

كَذَّبَتْ ثَمُودُ بِطَغْوَاهَآ ﴿١١﴾

11. Kaththabat thamoodu bitaghwaha

11 Thamud (people) denied (their Prophet) through their transgression (by rejecting the true Faith of Islamic Monotheism, and by following polytheism, and by committing every kind of sin).

		أَشْقَاهَا	انبَعَثَ	إِذِ
		ashqaha	inbaAAatha	Ithi
		The most wicked among them	Went forth	When

إِذِ انبَعَثَ أَشْقَاهَا ﴿١٢﴾

12. Ithi inbaAAatha ashqaha

12 When the most wicked man among them went forth (to kill the she-camel).

فَقَالَ	لَهُمْ	رَسُولُ	اللَّهِ	نَاقَةَ	اللَّهِ
Faqala	lahum	rasoolu	Allahi	naqata	Allahi
But said	To them	The Messenger	(of) Allah	(that is) the she camel	(of) Allah

وَسُقْيَاهَا
wasuqyaha
And (bar it from not having) its drink

فَقَالَ لَهُمْ رَسُولُ ٱللَّهِ نَاقَةَ ٱللَّهِ وَسُقْيَـٰهَا ۝

13. Faqala lahum rasoolu Allahi naqata Allahi wasuqyaha

13 But the Messenger of Allah [Salih (Saleh)] said to them: "Be cautious! Fear the evil end. That is the she-camel of Allah! (Do not harm it) and bar it not from having its drink!"

بِذَنبِهِمْ	رَبُّهُمْ	عَلَيْهِمْ	فَدَمْدَمَ	فَعَقَرُوهَا	فَكَذَّبُوهُ
bithanbihim	rabbuhum	AAalayhim	fadamdama	faAAaqarooha	Fakaththaboohu
Because of their sin	Their Lord	Them	So destroyed	They killed/ hamstrung it	Then they denied him

فَسَوَّاهَا
fasawwaha
And made them equal in destruction

فَكَذَّبُوهُ فَعَقَرُوهَا فَدَمْدَمَ عَلَيْهِمْ رَبُّهُم بِذَنۢبِهِمْ فَسَوَّىٰهَا ۝

14. Fakaththaboohu faAAaqarooha fadamdama AAalayhim rabbuhum bithanbihim fasawwaha

14 Then they denied him and they killed it. So their Lord destroyed them because of their sin, and made them equal in destruction (i.e. all grades of people, rich and poor, strong and weak, etc.)!

			عُقْبَاهَا	يَخَافُ	وَلَا
			AAuqbaha	yakhafu	Wala
			The consequences thereof	He feared	And not

وَلَا يَخَافُ عُقْبَـٰهَا ۝

15. Wala yakhafu AAuqbaha
15 And He (Allah) feared not the consequences thereof.

Surah # 92
AL-LAIL

Makkia

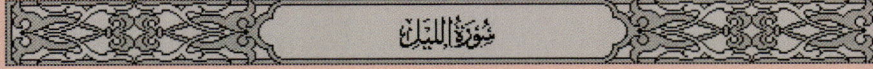

Verses 21

Sections 1

بِسْمِ اللهِ الرَّحْمٰنِ الرَّحِيمِ

			يَغْشَى	إِذَا	وَٱلَّيْلِ
			Yaghsha	itha	Waallayli
			It envelops	When/ as	By the night

﴿ وَٱلَّيْلِ إِذَا يَغْشَىٰ ۝ ﴾

1. Wa**a**llayli i**t**ha yaghsha

1 By the night as it envelops;

			تَجَلَّى	إِذَا	وَٱلنَّهَارِ
			tajalla	itha	Waalnnahari
			It appears in brightness	As/ when	And by the day

وَٱلنَّهَارِ إِذَا تَجَلَّىٰ ۝

2. Wa**a**lnnahari i**t**ha tajall**a**

2 And by the day as it appears in brightness;

		وَٱلْأُنثَى	ٱلذَّكَرَ	خَلَقَ	وَمَا
		waal-ontha	Alththakara	khalaqa	Wama
		And female	Male	Who created	And by him

وَمَا خَلَقَ ٱلذَّكَرَ وَٱلْأُنثَىٰ ۝

3. Wam**a** khalaqa al**th**thakara waal-onth**a**

3 And by Him Who created male and female;

				لَشَتَّىٰ	سَعْيَكُمْ	إِنَّ
				lashatta	saAAyakum	Inna
				(are) indeed diverse	Your efforts	Certainly

إِنَّ سَعْيَكُمْ لَشَتَّىٰ ٤

4. Inna saAAyakum lashatta

4 Certainly, your efforts and deeds are diverse (different in aims and purposes);

			وَاتَّقَىٰ	أَعْطَىٰ	مَن	فَأَمَّا
			waittaqa	aAAta	man	Faamma
			And fears Him (the best)	Gives	him who	As for

فَأَمَّا مَنْ أَعْطَىٰ وَاتَّقَىٰ ٥

5. Faamma man aAAta waittaqa

5 As for him who gives (in charity) and keeps his duty to Allah and fears Him,

				بِالْحُسْنَىٰ	وَصَدَّقَ
				bialhusna	Wasaddaqa
				In the best	And believes

وَصَدَّقَ بِالْحُسْنَىٰ ٦

6. Wasaddaqa bialhusna

6 And believes in *Al-Husna*.

				لِلْيُسْرَىٰ	فَسَنُيَسِّرُهُ
				lilyusra	Fasanuyassiruhu
				(the) path of ease	We will make smooth for him

فَسَنُيَسِّرُهُ لِلْيُسْرَىٰ ٧

7. Fasanuyassiruhu lilyusra

7 We will make smooth for him the path of ease (goodness).

		وَاسْتَغْنَىٰ	بَخِلَ	مَن	وَأَمَّا
		waistaghna	bakhila	man	Waamma

		And thinks himself self-sufficient	Is a miser	He who	And but

$$وَأَمَّا مَنْ بَخِلَ وَٱسْتَغْنَىٰ ۝$$

8. Waamma man bakhila waistaghna
8 But he who is greedy miser and thinks himself self-sufficient.

				بِالْحُسْنَىٰ	وَكَذَّبَ
				bialhusna	Wakaththaba
				The best	And deines

$$وَكَذَّبَ بِٱلْحُسْنَىٰ ۝$$

9. Wakaththaba bialhusna
9 And belies to *Al-Husna* (goodness)

				لِلْعُسْرَىٰ	فَسَنُيَسِّرُهُ
				lilAAusra	Fasanuyassiruhu
				(The path) of Evil	Then We will make smooth for him

$$فَسَنُيَسِّرُهُ لِلْعُسْرَىٰ ۝$$

10. Fasanuyassiruhu lilAAusra
10 We will make smooth for him the path for evil;

تَرَدَّىٰ	إِذَا	مَالُهُ	عَنْهُ	يُغْنِي	وَمَا
taradda	itha	maluhu	AAanhu	yughnee	Wama
He goes down	When	His wealth	Him	Will benefit	And what

$$وَمَا يُغْنِي عَنْهُ مَالُهُ إِذَا تَرَدَّىٰ ۝$$

11. Wama yughnee AAanhu maluhu itha taradda
11 And what will his wealth benefit him when he goes down (in destruction).

			لَلْهُدَى	عَلَيْنَا	إِنَّ
			lalhuda	AAalayna	Inna
			(is) the	On Us	Truly

			guidance

$$\text{إِنَّ عَلَيْنَا لَلْهُدَى ﴿١٢﴾}$$

12. Inna AAalayna lalhuda

12 Truly! Ours it is (to give) guidance,

وَالْأُولَى	لَلْآخِرَةَ	لَنَا	وَإِنَّ
waal-oola	lal-akhirata	lana	Wa-inna
And the first (this world)	(is) the last (hereafter)	Onto Us	And truly

$$\text{وَإِنَّ لَنَا لَلْآخِرَةَ وَالْأُولَى ﴿١٣﴾}$$

13. Wa-inna lana lal-akhirata waal-oola

13 And truly, unto Us (belong) the last (Hereafter) and the first (this world).

		تَلَظَّى	نَارًا	فَأَنْذَرْتُكُمْ
		talaththa	naran	Faanthartukum
		Blazing fiercely	(of) a fire	Therefore I Have warned you

$$\text{فَأَنْذَرْتُكُمْ نَارًا تَلَظَّى ﴿١٤﴾}$$

14. Faanthartukum naran talaththa

14 Therefore I have warned you of a Fire blazing fiercely (Hell);

الْأَشْقَى	إِلَّا	يَصْلَاهَا	لَا
al-ashqa	illa	yaslaha	La
The most wrentched	Save	Shall burn/enter in it	None

$$\text{لَا يَصْلَاهَا إِلَّا الْأَشْقَى ﴿١٥﴾}$$

15. La yaslaha illa al-ashqa

15 None shall enter it save the most wretched,

	وَتَوَلَّى	كَذَّبَ	الَّذِي
	watawalla	kaththaba	Allathee
	And turns away	Denies	Who

ٱلَّذِى كَذَّبَ وَتَوَلَّىٰ ۝

16. Allathee kaththaba watawalla

16 Who denies and turns away.

				الْأَتْقَى	وَسَيُجَنَّبُهَا
				al-atqa	Wasayujannabuha
				The pious	And will be far removed from it

وَسَيُجَنَّبُهَا ٱلْأَتْقَى ۝

17. Wasayujannabuha al-atqa

17 And *Al-Muttaqun* (the pious and righteous - see V.2:2) will be far removed from it (Hell).

		يَتَزَكَّىٰ	مَالَهُ	يُؤْتِى	الَّذِي
		yatazakka	malahu	yu/tee	Allathee
		That it may grow/increase	His wealth	Spends	He who

ٱلَّذِى يُؤْتِى مَالَهُۥ يَتَزَكَّىٰ ۝

18. Allathee yu/tee malahu yatazakka

18 He who spends his wealth for increase in self-purification,

تُجْزَىٰ	نِّعْمَةٍ	مِن	عِندَهُ	لِأَحَدٍ	وَمَا
tujza	niAAmatin	min	AAindahu	li-ahadin	Wama
To be paid back	Favour	Any	He has	For anyone	And not

وَمَا لِأَحَدٍ عِندَهُۥ مِن نِّعْمَةٍ تُجْزَىٰٓ ۝

19. Wama li-ahadin AAindahu min niAAmatin tujza

19 And have in his mind no favour from anyone for which a reward is expected in return,

الْأَعْلَى	رَبِّهِ	وَجْهِ	ابْتِغَاء	إِلَّا
al-aAAla	rabbihi	wajhi	ibtighaa	Illa
The Most High	(of) his Lord	The face	To seek	Except

إِلَّا ٱبْتِغَآءَ وَجْهِ رَبِّهِ ٱلْأَعْلَىٰ ﴿٢٠﴾

20. Illa ibtighaa wajhi rabbihi al-aAAla

20 Except only the desire to seek the Countenance of his Lord, the Most High;

				يَرْضَىٰ	وَلَسَوْفَ
				yarda	Walasawfa
				He will be pleased	And surely will

وَلَسَوْفَ يَرْضَىٰ ﴿٢١﴾

21. Walasawfa yarda

21 He surely will be pleased (when he will enter Paradise).

Surah # 93
AD-DHUAH

Makkia

سُورَةُ الضُّحَىٰ

Verses 11
Sections 1

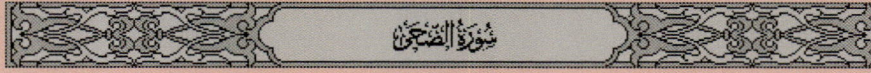

					وَالضُّحَىٰ
					Waaldduha
					By the forenoon

﴿ وَٱلضُّحَىٰ ١ ﴾

1. Waaldduha

1 By the forenoon (after sun-rise);

			سَجَىٰ	إِذَا	وَٱللَّيْلِ
			saja	itha	Waallayli
			It still	When	By the night

109

وَٱلَّيْلِ إِذَا سَجَىٰ ﴿٢﴾

2. Waallayli itha saja
2 And by the night when it is still (or darkens);

قَلَىٰ	وَمَا	رَبُّكَ	وَدَّعَكَ	مَا
qala	wama	rabbuka	waddaAAaka	Ma
Hated you	Nor	Your Lord	Has forsaken you	Neither

مَا وَدَّعَكَ رَبُّكَ وَمَا قَلَىٰ ﴿٣﴾

3. Ma waddaAAaka rabbuka wama qala
3 Your Lord (O Muhammad (ﷺ)) has neither forsaken you nor hated you.

الْأُولَىٰ	مِنَ	لَكَ	خَيْرٌ	وَلَلْآخِرَةُ
al-oola	mina	laka	khayrun	Walal-akhiratu
The first (world)	Than	For you	(is) better	And indeed the (hereafter)

وَلَلْآخِرَةُ خَيْرٌ لَّكَ مِنَ ٱلْأُولَىٰ ﴿٤﴾

4. Walal-akhiratu khayrun laka mina al-oola
4 And indeed the Hereafter is better for you than the present (life of this world).

		فَتَرْضَىٰ	رَبُّكَ	يُعْطِيكَ	وَلَسَوْفَ
		fatarda	rabbuka	yuAAteeka	Walasawfa
		So that you shall be well pleased	Your Lord	Will give you	And verily

وَلَسَوْفَ يُعْطِيكَ رَبُّكَ فَتَرْضَىٰ ﴿٥﴾

5. Walasawfa yuAAteeka rabbuka fatarda
5 And verily, your Lord will give you (all i.e. good) so that you shall be well-pleased.

		فَآوَىٰ	يَتِيمًا	يَجِدْكَ	أَلَمْ
		faawa	yateeman	yajidka	Alam

		So He gave you refuge	An orphan	He find you	Did not

أَلَمْ يَجِدْكَ يَتِيمًا فَآوَىٰ ۝

6. Alam yajidka yateeman fa<u>a</u>w<u>a</u>

6 Did He not find you (O Muhammad (ﷺ)) an orphan and gave you a refuge?

		فَهَدَىٰ	ضَالًّا	وَوَجَدَكَ
		fahad<u>a</u>	<u>d</u>all<u>a</u>n	Wawajadaka
		So He guided you	Unaware	So He found you

وَوَجَدَكَ ضَآلًّا فَهَدَىٰ ۝

7. Wawajadaka <u>d</u>all<u>a</u>n fahad<u>a</u>

7 And He found you unaware (of the Qur'an, its legal laws, and Prophethood, etc.) and guided you?

		فَأَغْنَىٰ	عَائِلًا	وَوَجَدَكَ
		fa<u>a</u>ghn<u>a</u>	AA<u>a</u>-ilan	Wawajadaka
		So He made you rich	Poor	And He found you

وَوَجَدَكَ عَآئِلًا فَأَغْنَىٰ ۝

8. Wawajadaka AA<u>a</u>-ilan fa<u>a</u>ghn<u>a</u>

8 And He found you poor, and made you rich (selfsufficient with selfcontentment, etc.)?

		تَقْهَرْ	فَلَا	الْيَتِيمَ	فَأَمَّا
		taqhar	fal<u>a</u>	alyateema	Faamm<u>a</u>
		Treat with oppression	Not	The orphan	As for

فَأَمَّا الْيَتِيمَ فَلَا تَقْهَرْ ۝

9. Faamm<u>a</u> alyateema fal<u>a</u> taqhar

9 Therefore, treat not the orphan with oppression,

		تَنْهَرْ	فَلَا	السَّائِلَ	وَأَمَّا
		Tanhar	fal<u>a</u>	alss<u>a</u>-ila	Waamm<u>a</u>
		Repulse	Not	The beggar	And as for

وَأَمَّا ٱلسَّآئِلَ فَلَا تَنْهَر ۝

10. Waamma alssa-ila fala tanhar

10 And repulse not the beggar;

		فَحَدِّثْ	رَبِّكَ	بِنِعْمَةِ	وَأَمَّا
		Fahaddith	rabbika	biniAAmati	Waamma
		So proclaim	(of) your Lord	the grace	And as for

وَأَمَّا بِنِعْمَةِ رَبِّكَ فَحَدِّثْ ۝

11. Waamma biniAAmati rabbika fahaddith

11 And proclaim the Grace of your Lord (i.e. the Prophethood and all other Graces).

Surah # 94
AL-INSHIRAH

Makkia

Verses 8

Sections 1

بِسْمِ ٱللَّهِ ٱلرَّحْمَٰنِ ٱلرَّحِيمِ

		صَدْرَكَ	لَكَ	نَشْرَحْ	أَلَمْ
		sadraka	laka	nashrah	Alam
		Your breast	For you	We opened	Have not

أَلَمْ نَشْرَحْ لَكَ صَدْرَكَ ۝

1. Alam nashrah laka sadraka

1 Have We not opened your breast for you (O Muhammad ﷺ)?

		وِزْرَكَ	عَنكَ	وَوَضَعْنَا
		wizraka	AAanka	WawadaAAna
		Your burden	Form you	And removed

112

$$\text{وَوَضَعْنَا عَنكَ وِزْرَكَ} \ \textcircled{\scriptsize ٢}$$

2. WawadaAAna AAanka wizraka

2 And removed from you your burden,

			Thahraka	anqada	Allathee
			ظَهْرَكَ	أَنقَضَ	الَّذِي
			Your back	Weighed down	Which

$$\text{الَّذِىٓ أَنقَضَ ظَهْرَكَ} \ \textcircled{\scriptsize ٣}$$

3. Allathee anqada thahraka

3 Which weighed down your back?

			thikraka	laka	WarafaAAna
			ذِكْرَكَ	لَكَ	وَرَفَعْنَا
			Your mention	For you	And raised high

$$\text{وَرَفَعْنَا لَكَ ذِكْرَكَ} \ \textcircled{\scriptsize ٤}$$

4. WarafaAAna laka thikraka

4 And raised high your fame/ your mention?

		yusran	alAAusri	maAAa	Fa-inna
		يُسْرًا	الْعُسْرِ	مَعَ	فَإِنَّ
		(is) relief	The Hardship	With	So verily

$$\text{فَإِنَّ مَعَ ٱلْعُسْرِ يُسْرًا} \ \textcircled{\scriptsize ٥}$$

5. Fa-inna maAAa alAAusri yusran

5 So verily, with the hardship, there is relief,

		yusran	alAAusri	maAAa	Inna
		يُسْرًا	الْعُسْرِ	مَعَ	إِنَّ
		(is) relief	The hardship	With	Verily

$$\text{إِنَّ مَعَ ٱلْعُسْرِ يُسْرًا} \ \textcircled{\scriptsize ٦}$$

6. Inna maAAa alAAusri yusran

6 Verily, with the hardship, there is relief (i.e. there is one hardship with two reliefs, so one hardship cannot overcome two reliefs).

			فَانصَبْ	فَرَغْتَ	فَإِذَا
			fainṣab	faraghta	Fa-itha
			Then stand up (for Allah's worship)	You have finished (your work)	So when

فَإِذَا فَرَغْتَ فَٱنصَبْ ۝

7. Fa-itha faraghta fainṣab

7 So when you have finished (from your occupation), then stand up for Allah's worship (i.e. stand up for prayer).

			فَارْغَب	رَّبِّكَ	وَإِلَى
			fairghab	rabbika	Wa-ila
			Turn (your invocation)	Your Lord	And to

وَإِلَى رَبِّكَ فَٱرْغَب ۝

8. Wa-ila rabbika fairghab

8 And to your Lord (Alone) turn (all your intentions and hopes and) your invocations.

Surah # 95
AT-TEEN

Makkia

سُورَةُ التِّينِ

Verses 8
Sections 1

بِسْمِ اللهِ الرَّحْمَنِ الرَّحِيمِ

				وَالزَّيْتُونِ	وَالتِّينِ
				waalzzaytooni	Waaltteeni
				And the Olive	By the fig

114

وَٱلتِّينِ وَٱلزَّيْتُونِ ﴿١﴾

1. Waaltteeni waalzzaytooni
1 By the fig, and the olive,

				seeneena	Watoori
				(of) Sinai	And the Mount

وَطُورِ سِينِينَ ﴿٢﴾

2. Watoori seeneena
2 By Mount Sinai,

			al-ameeni	albaladi	Wahatha
			(of) security	City	And this

وَهَـٰذَا ٱلْبَلَدِ ٱلْأَمِينِ ﴿٣﴾

3. Wahatha albaladi al-ameeni
3 And by this city of security (Makkah),

taqweemin	ahsani	fee	al-insana	khalaqna	Laqad
Stature	The best	In	Man	We created	Verily

لَقَدْ خَلَقْنَا ٱلْإِنسَـٰنَ فِىٓ أَحْسَنِ تَقْوِيمٍ ﴿٤﴾

4. Laqad khalaqna al-insana fee ahsani taqweemin
4 Verily, We created man of the best stature (mould),

		safileena	asfala	radadnahu	Thumma
		(of) the Low	To the lowest	We reduced him	Then

ثُمَّ رَدَدْنَـٰهُ أَسْفَلَ سَـٰفِلِينَ ﴿٥﴾

5. Thumma radadnahu asfala safileena

5 Then We reduced him to the lowest of the low,

فَلَهُمْ	الصَّالِحَاتِ	وَعَمِلُوا	آمَنُوا	الَّذِينَ	إِلَّا
falahum	alssalihati	waAAamiloo	amanoo	allatheena	Illa
Then for them (will be)	Righteous deeds	And do	Believe	Those who	Save

			مَمْنُونٍ	غَيْرُ	أَجْرٌ
			mamnoonin	ghayru	ajrun
			End	Without	A reward

إِلَّا ٱلَّذِينَ ءَامَنُوا۟ وَعَمِلُوا۟ ٱلصَّـٰلِحَـٰتِ فَلَهُمْ أَجْرٌ غَيْرُ مَمْنُونٍ ۝

6. Illa allatheena amanoo waAAamiloo alssalihati falahum ajrun ghayru mamnoonin

6 Save those who believe (in Islamic Monotheism) and do righteous deeds, then they shall have a reward without end (Paradise).

		بِالدِّينِ	بَعْدُ	يُكَذِّبُكَ	فَمَا
		Bid-deen	baadu	yukazibuka	fama
		The say of Resurrection	after	You deny	Then how

فَمَا يُكَذِّبُكَ بَعْدُ بِٱلدِّينِ ۝

Then what (or how) causes you (O disbelievers) to deny the Recompense (i.e. Day of Resurrection)?

		الْحَاكِمِينَ	بِأَحْكَمِ	اللَّهُ	أَلَيْسَ
		alhakimeena	bi-ahkami	Allahu	Alaysa
		(of the judges)	The best	Allah	Is not

أَلَيْسَ ٱللَّهُ بِأَحْكَمِ ٱلْحَـٰكِمِينَ ۝

8. Alaysa Allahu bi-ahkami alhakimeena

Is not Allah the Best of judges?

Surah # 96
AL-ALAQ

سُورَةُ الْعَلَق

Verses 19
Sections 1

بِسْمِ اللهِ الرَّحْمنِ الرَّحِيمِ

خَلَقَ	الَّذِي	رَبِّكَ	بِاسْمِ	اقْرَأْ
khalaqa	allathee	rabbika	bi-ismi	Iqra/
Created	Who	(of) your Lord	In the name	read

﴿ اقْرَأْ بِاسْمِ رَبِّكَ الَّذِي خَلَقَ ۝ ﴾

1. Iqra/ bi-ismi rabbika allathee khalaqa

Read! In the Name of your Lord, Who has created (all that exists),

	عَلَقٍ	مِنْ	الْإِنسَانَ	خَلَقَ
	AAalaqin	min	al-insana	Khalaqa
	A clot	From	Man	He created

خَلَقَ الْإِنسَانَ مِنْ عَلَقٍ ۝

2. Khalaqa al-insana min AAalaqin

Has created man from a clot (a piece of thick coagulated blood).

		الْأَكْرَمُ	وَرَبُّكَ	اقْرَأْ
		al-akramu	warabbuka	Iqra/
		(is) the most generous	And your Lord	Read

اقْرَأْ وَرَبُّكَ الْأَكْرَمُ ۝

3. Iqra/ warabbuka al-akramu

Read! And your Lord is the Most Generous,

		بِالْقَلَمِ	عَلَّمَ	الَّذِي
		bialqalami	AAallama	Allathee
		By the pen	Has taught	Who

117

$$ \text{ٱلَّذِى عَلَّمَ بِٱلْقَلَمِ} \ ۝ $$

4. Allathee AAallama bialqalami
Who has taught (the writing) by the pen [the first person to write was Prophet Idrees (Enoch)],

يَعْلَمْ	لَمْ	مَا	ٱلْإِنسَانَ	عَلَّمَ
yaAAlam	lam	ma	al-ins**a**na	AAallama
He knew	Not	That which	Man	He has taught

$$ \text{عَلَّمَ ٱلْإِنسَٰنَ مَا لَمْ يَعْلَمْ} \ ۝ $$

5. AAallama al-insa**na m**a** lam yaAAlam**
He has taught man that which he knew not.

لَيَطْغَى		ٱلْإِنسَانَ	إِنَّ	كَلَّا
layatgh**a**		al-ins**a**na	inna	Kall**a**
Does transgress		Man	Verily	Nay

$$ \text{كَلَّا إِنَّ ٱلْإِنسَٰنَ لَيَطْغَىٰ} \ ۝ $$

6. Kalla** inna al-ins**a**na layatgh**a****
Nay! Verily, man does transgress all bounds (in disbelief and evil deed, etc.).

		ٱسْتَغْنَى	رَّآهُ	أَن
		istaghn**a**	ra**a**hu	An
		Self-sufficient	He considers himself	Because

$$ \text{أَن رَّءَاهُ ٱسْتَغْنَىٰ} \ ۝ $$

7. An raa**hu istaghn**a****
Because he considers himself self-sufficient.

الرُّجْعَى	رَّبِّكَ	إِلَى	إِنَّ
alrruj**A**A**a**	Rabbika	il**a**	Inna
(is) the return	Your Lord	Unto	Surely

118

$$\text{إِنَّ إِلَىٰ رَبِّكَ ٱلرُّجْعَىٰ ۝}$$

8. Inna ila rabbika alrrujAAa

Surely! Unto your Lord is the return.

			يَنْهَى	ٱلَّذِي	أَرَأَيْتَ
			yanha	allathee	Araayta
			Prevents	Him who	Have you seen

$$\text{أَرَءَيْتَ ٱلَّذِى يَنْهَىٰ ۝}$$

9. Araayta allathee yanha

Have you (O Muhammad (ﷺ)) seen him (i.e. Abu Jahl) who prevents,

			صَلَّى	إِذَا	عَبْدًا
			Salla	itha	AAabdan
			He prays	When	A slave

$$\text{عَبْدًا إِذَا صَلَّىٰ ۝}$$

10. AAabdan itha salla

A slave (Muhammad (ﷺ)) when he prays?

الْهُدَى	عَلَى	كَانَ	إِن	أَرَأَيْتَ
alhuda	AAala	Kana	in	Araayta
The guidance	On	He is	If	Have you seen

$$\text{أَرَءَيْتَ إِن كَانَ عَلَى ٱلْهُدَىٰ ۝}$$

11. Araayta in kana AAala alhuda

Tell me, if he (Muhammad (ﷺ)) is on the guidance (of Allah)?

			بِالتَّقْوَى	أَمَرَ	أَوْ
			bialttaqwa	amara	Aw
			Piety	Enjoins	Or

أَوْ أَمَرَ بِٱلتَّقْوَىٰ ﴿١٢﴾

12. Aw amara bialttaqwa
Or enjoins piety?

		وَتَوَلَّىٰ	كَذَّبَ	إِن	أَرَأَيْتَ
		watawalla	kaththaba	in	Araayta
		And turns away	He denies	If	Have you seen

أَرَءَيْتَ إِن كَذَّبَ وَتَوَلَّىٰ ﴿١٣﴾

13. Araayta in kaththaba watawalla
Tell me if he (the disbeliever, Abu Jahl) denies (the truth, i.e. this Qur'an), and turns away?

	يَرَىٰ	ٱللَّهَ	بِأَنَّ	يَعْلَم	أَلَمْ
	yara	Allaha	bi-anna	yaAAlam	Alam
	Sees	Allah	That	He know	Does not

أَلَمْ يَعْلَم بِأَنَّ ٱللَّهَ يَرَىٰ ﴿١٤﴾

14. Alam yaAAlam bi-anna Allaha yara
Knows he not that Allah does see (what he does)?

بِٱلنَّاصِيَةِ	لَنَسْفَعًا	يَنتَهِ	لَّمْ	لَئِن	كَلَّا
bialnnasiyati	lanasfaAAan	yantahi	lam	la-in	Kalla
By the forelock	We will catch him	He ceases	Not	If	Nay

كَلَّا لَئِن لَّمْ يَنتَهِ لَنَسْفَعًا بِٱلنَّاصِيَةِ ﴿١٥﴾

15. Kalla la-in lam yantahi lanasfaAAan bialnnasiyati
Nay! If he (Abu Jahl) ceases not, We will catch him by the forelock,

			خَاطِئَةٍ	كَاذِبَةٍ	نَاصِيَةٍ
			khati-atin	kathibatin	Nasiyatin
			Sinful	A lying	Forelock

نَاصِيَةٍ كَاذِبَةٍ خَاطِئَةٍ ۝

16. Nasiyatin kathibatin khati-atin
A lying, sinful forelock!

				نَادِيَه	فَلْيَدْعُ
				nadiyahu	FalyadAAu
				His council	Then let him call upon

فَلْيَدْعُ نَادِيَهُ ۝

17. FalyadAAu nadiyahu
Then, let him call upon his council (of helpers),

				الزَّبَانِيَةَ	سَنَدْعُ
				alzzabaniyata	SanadAAu
				The gaurds of Hell	We will call out

سَنَدْعُ ٱلزَّبَانِيَةَ ۝

18. SanadAAu alzzabaniyata
We will call the guards of Hell (to deal with him)!

وَٱقْتَرِب	وَٱسْجُدْ	تُطِعْهُ	لَا	كَلَّا
waiqtarib	waosjud	tutiAAhu	La	Kalla
And drew near (to Allah)	And fall prostrate	Obey Him	Do not	Nay

كَلَّا لَا تُطِعْهُ وَٱسْجُدْ وَٱقْتَرِب ۩ ۝

19. Kalla la tutiAAhu waosjud waiqtarib
Nay! (O Muhammad (ﷺ))! Do not obey him (Abu Jahl). Fall prostrate and draw near to Allah! (Sajda-e-Tilawath)

Surah # 97
AL-QADR

Makkia

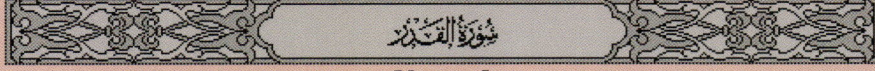

Verses 5

Sections 1

بِسْمِ اللهِ الرَّحْمَنِ الرَّحِيمِ

الْقَدْرِ	لَيْلَةٍ	فِي	أَنزَلْنَاهُ	إِنَّا
alqadri	laylati	fee	anzalnahu	Inna
Decree	(is) the night of	In	Have sent it down	Verily we

إِنَّا أَنزَلْنَاهُ فِي لَيْلَةِ ٱلْقَدْرِ ۝

1. Inna anzalnahu fee laylati alqadri
Verily! We have sent it (this Qur'an) down in the night of *Al-Qadr* (Decree)

الْقَدْرِ	لَيْلَةُ	مَا	أَدْرَاكَ	وَمَا
alqadri	laylatu	ma	adraka	Wama
(of) decree	The night	What	Will make you know	And what

وَمَآ أَدْرَىٰكَ مَا لَيْلَةُ ٱلْقَدْرِ ۝

2. Wama adraka ma laylatu alqadri
And what will make you know what the night of *Al-Qadr* (Decree) is?

شَهْرٍ	أَلْفِ	مِّنْ	خَيْرٌ	الْقَدْرِ	لَيْلَةُ
shahrin	Alfi	min	khayrun	alqadri	Laylatu
Months	A thousand	Than	(is) better	(of) decree	The night

لَيْلَةُ ٱلْقَدْرِ خَيْرٌ مِّنْ أَلْفِ شَهْرٍ ۝

3. Laylatu alqadri khayrun min alfi shahrin
The night of *Al-Qadr* (Decree) is better than a thousand months (i.e. worshipping Allah in that night is better than worshipping Him a thousand months, i.e. 83 years and 4 months).

ربِّهم	بِإِذْنِ	فِيهَا	وَالرُّوحُ	الْمَلَائِكَةُ	تَنَزَّلُ
rabbihim	bi-ithni	feeha	waalrroohu	almala-ikatu	Tanazzalu
(of their Lord	By permission	Therein	And the spirit (Gabriel)	The angels	Descend

			أَمْرٍ	كُلِّ	مِّن
			amrin	kulli	min
			Decrees	All	With

$$\text{تَنَزَّلُ ٱلْمَلَٰٓئِكَةُ وَٱلرُّوحُ فِيهَا بِإِذْنِ رَبِّهِم مِّن كُلِّ أَمْرٍ ۝}$$

4. Tanazzalu almala-ikatu waalrroohu feeha bi-ithni rabbihim min kulli amrin

Therein descend the angels and the *Ruh* [Jibrael (Gabriel)] by Allah's Permission with all Decrees,

الْفَجْرِ	مَطْلَعِ	حَتَّىٰ	هِيَ	سَلَامٌ
alfajri	matlaAAi	hatta	hiya	Salamun
(of) dawn	The appearance	untill	(it) in	(there is) peace

$$\text{سَلَٰمٌ هِىَ حَتَّىٰ مَطْلَعِ ٱلْفَجْرِ ۝}$$

5. Salamun hiya hatta matlaAAi alfajri

Peace! (All that night, there is Peace and Goodness from Allah to His believing slaves) until the appearance of dawn.

Surah # 98
AL-BAIYYINAH

Makkia/ Madania

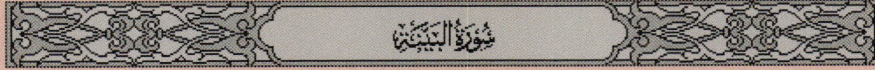

سُورَةُ البَيِّنَة

Verses 8
Sections 1

بِسْمِ اللهِ الرَّحْمٰنِ الرَّحِيمِ

أَهْلِ	مِنْ	كَفَرُوا	الَّذِينَ	يَكُنِ	لَمْ
ahli	min	Kafaroo	allatheena	yakuni	Lam
The people	From among	Disbelieve	Those who	Were	Not

الْبَيِّنَةُ	تَأْتِيَهُمُ	حَتَّى	مُنفَكِّينَ	وَالْمُشْرِكِينَ	الْكِتَابِ
albayyina**tu**	ta/tiyahumu	hatta	munfakkeena	waa**l**mushrikeena	alkit**a**bi
Clear evidence	Came to them	Until	Going to leave (their disbelief)	And the polytheists	(of) the scripture

لَمْ يَكُنِ ٱلَّذِينَ كَفَرُوا۟ مِنْ أَهْلِ ٱلْكِتَٰبِ وَٱلْمُشْرِكِينَ مُنفَكِّينَ حَتَّىٰ تَأْتِيَهُمُ ٱلْبَيِّنَةُ ﴿١﴾

1. Lam yakuni allatheena kafaroo min ahli alkit**a**bi waa**l**mushrikeena munfakkeena **h**att**a** ta/tiyahumu albayyina**tu**

Those who disbelieve from among the people of the Scripture (Jews and Christians) and among *Al-Mushrikun,* were not going to leave (their disbelief) until there came to them clear evidence.

مُطَهَّرَةً	صُحُفًا	يَتْلُو	اللَّهِ	مِّنَ	رَسُولٌ
mu**t**ahhara**tan**	**s**u**h**ufan	yatloo	All**a**hi	mina	Rasoolun
Purified	Pages	Recieting	Allah	From	A messenger

رَسُولٌ مِّنَ ٱللَّهِ يَتْلُوا۟ صُحُفًا مُّطَهَّرَةً ﴿٢﴾

2. Rasoolun mina Allahi yatloo su**h**ufan mu**t**ahhara**tan**

A Messenger (Muhammad (ﷺ)) from Allah, reciting (the Qur'an) purified pages [purified from *Al-Batil* (falsehood, etc.)].

			قَيِّمَةٌ	كُتُبٌ	فِيهَا
			qayyima**tun**	kutubun	Feeh**a**
			Correct and straight	(are) laws	Wherein

فِيهَا كُتُبٌ قَيِّمَةٌ ﴿٣﴾

3. Feeha kutubun qayyima**tun**

Containing correct and straight laws from Allah.

إِلَّا	الْكِتَابَ	أُوتُوا	الَّذِينَ	تَفَرَّقَ	وَمَا
ill**a**	alkit**a**ba	ootoo	alla**th**eena	tafarraqa	Wam**a**

124

Until	The scripture	Were given	Those who	Differed	And not
الْبَيِّنَةُ	جَاءَتْهُمُ	مَا	بَعْدِ		مِنْ
albayyina**tu**	jaat-humu	**ma**	baAAdi		min
Clear evidence	Came to them	that		agter	

وَمَا تَفَرَّقَ ٱلَّذِينَ أُوتُواْ ٱلْكِتَـٰبَ إِلَّا مِنْ بَعْدِ مَا جَاءَتْهُمُ ٱلْبَيِّنَةُ ﴿٤﴾

4. Wam**a** tafarraqa alla**th**eena ootoo alkit**a**ba ill**a** min baAAdi m**a** jaat-humu albayyina**tu**

And the people of the Scripture (Jews and Christians) differed not until after there came to them clear evidence. (i.e. Prophet Muhammad (ﷺ) and whatever was revealed to him).

mukhliseena	Allaha	liyaAAbudoo	illa	omiroo	Wama
مُخْلِصِينَ	ٱللَّهَ	لِيَعْبُدُواْ	إِلَّا	أُمِرُواْ	وَمَا
Making	Allah	That they should worship	But	They were commanded	And not
وَيُؤْتُوا	ٱلصَّلَاةَ	وَيُقِيمُوا	حُنَفَاءَ	ٱلدِّينَ	لَهُ
wayu/too	alssalata	wayuqeemoo	hunafaa	alddeena	lahu
And give	Prayer	And perform	Being upright	Faith, religion	To Him (Allah)
		ٱلْقَيِّمَةِ	دِينُ	وَذَٰلِكَ	ٱلزَّكَاةَ
		alqayyima**ti**	deenu	wa**th**alika	alzzak**a**ta
		(of) rightness	(is) the religion	And that	Zakat

وَمَا أُمِرُوٓاْ إِلَّا لِيَعْبُدُواْ ٱللَّهَ مُخْلِصِينَ لَهُ ٱلدِّينَ حُنَفَآءَ وَيُقِيمُواْ ٱلصَّلَوٰةَ وَيُؤْتُواْ ٱلزَّكَوٰةَ ۚ وَذَٰلِكَ دِينُ ٱلْقَيِّمَةِ ﴿٥﴾

5. Wam**a** omiroo ill**a** liyaAAbudoo All**a**ha mukhli**s**eena lahu alddeena **h**unaf**a**a wayuqeemoo alssal**a**ta wayu/too alzzak**a**ta wa**th**alika deenu alqayyima**ti**

And they were commanded not, but that they should worship Allah, and worship none but Him Alone (abstaining from ascribing partners to Him), and perform As-Salat (Iqamat-as-Salat) and give Zakat: and that is the right religion.

Verse 6

الْكِتَاب	أَهْلِ	مِنْ	كَفَرُوا	الَّذِينَ	إِنَّ
alkitabi	ahli	Min	kafaroo	allatheena	Inna
(of) the scripture	The people	From among	Who disbelieve	Those	Verily

فِيهَا	خَالِدِينَ	جَهَنَّمَ	نَارِ	فِي	وَالْمُشْرِكِينَ
feeha	khalideena	jahannama	nari	fee	waalmushrikeena
Therin	They will abide	(of) Hell	The fire	(will be) in	And the polytheists

		الْبَرِيَّةِ	شَرُّ	هُمْ	أُوْلَٰئِكَ
		albariyyati	sharru	hum	ola-ika
		(of) creatures	The worst	(they) are	They

إِنَّ ٱلَّذِينَ كَفَرُواْ مِنْ أَهْلِ ٱلْكِتَٰبِ وَٱلْمُشْرِكِينَ فِى نَارِ جَهَنَّمَ خَٰلِدِينَ فِيهَآ أُوْلَٰٓئِكَ هُمْ شَرُّ ٱلْبَرِيَّةِ ۝

6. Inna allatheena kafaroo min ahli alkitabi waalmushrikeena fee nari jahannama khalideena feeha ola-ika hum sharru albariyyati

Verily, those who disbelieve (in the religion of Islam, the Qur'an and Prophet Muhammad (ﷺ)) from among the people of the Scripture (Jews and Christians) and Al-Mushrikun will abide in the Fire of Hell. They are the worst of creatures.

Verse 7

أُوْلَٰئِكَ	الصَّالِحَاتِ	وَعَمِلُوا	آمَنُوا	الَّذِينَ	إِنَّ
ola-ika	alssalihati	waAAamiloo	amanoo	allatheena	Inna
They	Righteous good deeds	And do	Who believe	Those	Verily

		الْبَرِيَّةِ	خَيْرُ	هُمْ
		albariyyati	khayru	hum
		(of) creatures	The best	(they) are

إِنَّ ٱلَّذِينَ ءَامَنُواْ وَعَمِلُواْ ٱلصَّٰلِحَٰتِ أُوْلَٰٓئِكَ هُمْ خَيْرُ ٱلْبَرِيَّةِ ۝

7. Inna allatheena amanoo waAAamiloo alssalihati ola-ika hum khayru albariyyati

Verily, those who believe [in the Oneness of Allah, and in His Messenger Muhammad (ﷺ)) including all obligations ordered by Islam] and do righteous good deeds, they are the best of creatures.

جَزَاؤُهُمْ	عِندَ	رَبِّهِمْ	جَنَّاتُ	عَدْنٍ	تَجْرِي
Jazaohum	AAinda	Rabbihim	jannatu	AAadnin	tajree
Their reward	With	Their Lord	(is) Gardens	(of) (Eden) Eternity	Flowing

مِن	تَحْتِهَا	الْأَنْهَارُ	خَالِدِينَ	فِيهَا	أَبَدًا
min	tahtiha	al-anharu	khalideena	feeha	abadan
underneath		Rivers	They will abide	Therein	Forever

رَّضِيَ	اللَّهُ	عَنْهُمْ	وَرَضُوا	عَنْهُ	ذَلِكَ
radiya	Allahu	AAanhum	waradoo	AAanhu	thalika
Will be pleased	Allah	With them	And they will be pleased	with Him	That

لِمَنْ	خَشِيَ	رَبَّهُ			
liman	khashiya	rabbahu			
(is) for him who	Fears	His Lord			

جَزَاؤُهُمْ عِندَ رَبِّهِمْ جَنَّاتُ عَدْنٍ تَجْرِى مِن تَحْتِهَا ٱلْأَنْهَـٰرُ خَـٰلِدِينَ فِيهَآ أَبَدًا ۚ رَّضِىَ ٱللَّهُ عَنْهُمْ وَرَضُوا۟ عَنْهُ ۚ ذَٰلِكَ لِمَنْ خَشِىَ رَبَّهُۥ ۝

8. Jazaohum AAinda rabbihim jannatu AAadnin tajree min tahtiha al-anharu khalideena feeha abadan radiya Allahu AAanhum waradoo AAanhu thalika liman khashiya rabbahu

Their reward with their Lord is 'Adn (Eden) Paradise (Gardens of Eternity), underneath which rivers flow, they will abide therein forever, Allah Well-Pleased with them, and they with Him. That is for him who fears his Lord.

Surah # 99
AZ-ZALZALAH
Makkia/Madania

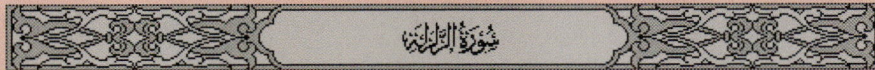

سُورَةُ الزَّلْزَلَةِ

Verses 8
Sections 1

بِسْمِ اللَّهِ الرَّحْمَنِ الرَّحِيمِ

		zilzalaha	al-ardu	zulzilati	Itha
		(with) its earthquake	The earth	Is shaken	When

$$\text{إِذَا زُلْزِلَتِ ٱلْأَرْضُ زِلْزَالَهَا ﴿١﴾}$$

1. Itha zulzilati al-ardu zilzalaha
When the earth is shaken with its (final) earthquake.

		athqalaha	al-ardu	Waakhrajati
		Its burden	The Earth	And throws out

$$\text{وَأَخْرَجَتِ ٱلْأَرْضُ أَثْقَالَهَا ﴿٢﴾}$$

2. Waakhrajati al-ardu athqalaha
And when the earth throws out its burdens,

		laha	ma	al-insanu	Waqala
		With it	What is the matter	Man	And will say

$$\text{وَقَالَ ٱلْإِنسَـٰنُ مَا لَهَا ﴿٣﴾}$$

3. Waqala al-insanu ma laha
And man will say: "What is the matter with it?"

		akhbaraha	tuhaddithu	Yawma-ithin
		Its information	It will declare	That day

$$\text{يَوْمَئِذٍ تُحَدِّثُ أَخْبَارَهَا ﴿٤﴾}$$

4. Yawma-ithin tuhaddithu akhbaraha
That Day it will declare its information (about all what happened over it of good or evil).

		لَهَا	أَوْحَى	رَبَّكَ	بِأَنَّ
		laha	awha	rabbaka	Bi-anna
		(for) it	Will inspire	Your Lord	Because

بِأَنَّ رَبَّكَ أَوْحَىٰ لَهَا ﴿٥﴾

5. Bi-anna rabbaka awha laha

Because your Lord has inspired it.

أَعْمَالَهُمْ	لِيُرَوْا	أَشْتَاتًا	النَّاسُ	يَصْدُرُ	يَوْمَئِذٍ
aAAmalahum	liyuraw	ashtatan	alnnasu	yasduru	Yawma-ithin
Their deeds	Then they may be shown	In scattered groups	Mankind	Will proceed	That day

يَوْمَئِذٍ يَصْدُرُ النَّاسُ أَشْتَاتًا لِّيُرَوْا أَعْمَالَهُمْ ﴿٦﴾

6. Yawma-ithin yasduru alnnasu ashtatan liyuraw aAAmalahum

That Day mankind will proceed in scattered groups that they may be shown their deeds.

يَرَهُ	خَيْرًا	ذَرَّةٍ	مِثْقَالَ	يَعْمَلْ	فَمَن
Yarahu	khayran	tharratin	mithqala	yaAAmal	Faman
Shall see it	Good	(of) an atom	Equal to the weight	Does	So whomsoever

فَمَن يَعْمَلْ مِثْقَالَ ذَرَّةٍ خَيْرًا يَرَهُ ﴿٧﴾

7. Faman yaAAmal mithqala tharratin khayran yarahu

So whosoever does good equal to the weight of an atom (or a small ant), shall see it.

يَرَهُ	شَرًّا	ذَرَّةٍ	مِثْقَالَ	يَعْمَلْ	وَمَن
yarahu	sharran	tharratin	mithqala	yaAAmal	Waman
Shall see it	Evil	(of) an atom	Equala to the weight	Does	And whomsoever

وَمَن يَعْمَلْ مِثْقَالَ ذَرَّةٍ شَرًّا يَرَهُ ﴿٨﴾

8. Waman yaAAmal mithqala tharratin sharran yarahu

And whosoever does evil equal to the weight of an atom (or a small ant), shall see it.

Surah # 100
AL-ADIYAT

Makkia/Madania

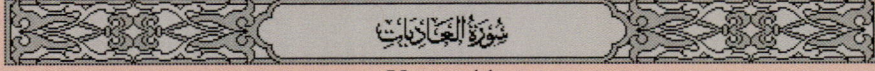

سُورَةُ الْعَادِيَاتِ

Verses 11
Sections 1

بِسْمِ اللهِ الرَّحْمٰنِ الرَّحِيمِ

				ضَبْحًا	وَالْعَادِيَاتِ
				<u>d</u>ab<u>h</u>an	WaalAA<u>a</u>diy<u>a</u>ti
				With painting	By the (steeds) that run

وَالْعَٰدِيَٰتِ ضَبْحًا ۝

1. WaalAA<u>a</u>diy<u>a</u>ti <u>d</u>ab<u>h</u>an

By the (steeds) that run, with panting (breath),

				قَدْحًا	فَالْمُورِيَاتِ
				qad<u>h</u>an	Faalmooriy<u>a</u>ti
				(with) a flint	Striking sparks of fire

فَالْمُورِيَٰتِ قَدْحًا ۝

2. Faalmooriy<u>a</u>ti qad<u>h</u>an

Striking sparks of fire (by their hooves),

				صُبْحًا	فَالْمُغِيرَاتِ
				<u>S</u>ub<u>h</u>an	Faalmugheer<u>a</u>ti
				At dawn	And scouring to the raids

130

$$\text{فَٱلْمُغِيرَاتِ صُبْحًا ﴿٣﴾}$$

3. Faalmugheerati subhan
And scouring to the raid at dawn

			نَقْعًا	بِهِ	فَأَثَرْنَ
			naqAAan	bihi	Faatharna
			Dust	In it	And they raise

$$\text{فَأَثَرْنَ بِهِ نَقْعًا ﴿٤﴾}$$

4. Faatharna bihi naqAAan
And raise the dust in clouds the while,

			جَمْعًا	بِهِ	فَوَسَطْنَ
			jamAAan	bihi	Fawasatna
			Into the midst (of the foe)	(with it)	And penetrate forthwith

$$\text{فَوَسَطْنَ بِهِ جَمْعًا ﴿٥﴾}$$

5. Fawasatna bihi jamAAan
Penetrating forthwith as one into the midst (of the foe);

		لَكَنُودٌ	لِرَبِّهِ	الْإِنسَانَ	إِنَّ
		lakanoodun	Lirabbihi	al-insana	Inna
		(is) ungreatful	To his Lord	Man	Verily

$$\text{إِنَّ ٱلْإِنسَانَ لِرَبِّهِ لَكَنُودٌ ﴿٦﴾}$$

6. Inna al-insana lirabbihi lakanoodun
Verily! Man (disbeliever) is ungrateful to his Lord;

		لَشَهِيدٌ	ذَلِكَ	عَلَى	وَإِنَّهُ
		Lashaheedun	thalika	AAala	Wa-innahu
		(is) witness	That	To	And verily he

$$\text{وَإِنَّهُ عَلَىٰ ذَٰلِكَ لَشَهِيدٌ ﴿٧﴾}$$

7. Wa-innahu AAala thalika lashaheedun

And to that fact he bears witness (by his deeds);

وَإِنَّهُ	لِحُبِّ	الْخَيْرِ	لَشَدِيدٌ		
Wa-innahu	lihubbi	alkhayri	lashadeedun		
And verily he	In the Love	(of) wealth	(is) violent		

$$\text{وَإِنَّهُ لِحُبِّ ٱلْخَيْرِ لَشَدِيدٌ ﴿٨﴾}$$

8. Wa-innahu lihubbi alkhayri lashadeedun

And verily, he is violent in the love of wealth.

أَفَلَا	يَعْلَمُ	إِذَا	بُعْثِرَ	مَا	فِي
Afala	yaAAlamu	itha	buAAthira	ma	fee
Does not	He know	When	Will be brought out	What/that	(is) in

الْقُبُورِ					
alquboori					
The graves					

$$\text{۞ أَفَلَا يَعْلَمُ إِذَا بُعْثِرَ مَا فِي ٱلْقُبُورِ ﴿٩﴾}$$

9. Afala yaAAlamu itha buAAthira ma fee alquboori

Knows he not that when the contents of the graves are brought out and poured forth (all mankind is resurrected).

وَحُصِّلَ	مَا	فِي	الصُّدُورِ		
Wahussila	ma	fee	alssudoori		
And shall be made known	Which/that	In	The breasts		

$$\text{وَحُصِّلَ مَا فِي ٱلصُّدُورِ ﴿١٠﴾}$$

10. Wahussila ma fee alssudoori

And that which is in the breasts (of men) shall be made known.

	لَّخَبِيرٌ	يَوْمَئِذٍ	بِهِمْ	رَّبَّهُم	إِنَّ
	lakhabee**run**	yawma-i**th**in	bihim	rabbahum	Inna
	(will be) well Acquinted	That day	With them	Their Lord	Verily

﴿ إِنَّ رَبَّهُم بِهِمْ يَوْمَئِذٍ لَّخَبِيرٌ ۝ ﴾

11. Inna rabbahum bihim yawma-ithin lakhabeerun
Verily, that Day (i.e. the Day of Resurrection) their Lord will be Well-Acquainted with them (as to their deeds), (and will reward them for their deeds).

Surah # 101
AL-QARIAH
Makkia

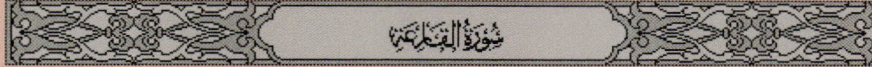

Verses 11
Sections 1

بِسْمِ اللَّهِ الرَّحْمَٰنِ الرَّحِيمِ

					الْقَارِعَةُ
					Alqa**ri**AAa**tu**
					The striking (Hour)

﴿ ٱلْقَارِعَةُ ۝ ﴾

1. AlqariAAatu
Al-Qari'ah (the striking Hour i.e. the Day of Resurrection),

				الْقَارِعَةُ	مَا
				alqa**ri**AAa**tu**	Ma
				(is) the striking (Hour)	What

مَا ٱلْقَارِعَةُ ۝

2. Ma alqariAAatu
What is the striking (Hour)?

		الْقَارِعَةُ	مَا	أَدْرَاكَ	وَمَا
		alqariAAatu	ma	Adraka	Wama
		The striking (Hour) (is)	What	Will make you know	And what

وَمَآ أَدْرَىٰكَ مَا ٱلْقَارِعَةُ ٣

3. Wama adraka ma alqariAAatu
And what will make you know what the striking (Hour) is?

الْمَبْثُوثِ	كَالْفَرَاشِ	النَّاسُ	يَكُونُ	يَوْمَ
almabthoothi	kaalfarashi	alnnasu	yakoonu	Yawma
Scattered about	Like moths	Mankind	Will be	(It is) the day (when)

يَوْمَ يَكُونُ ٱلنَّاسُ كَٱلْفَرَاشِ ٱلْمَبْثُوثِ ٤

4. Yawma yakoonu alnnasu kaalfarashi almabthoothi
It is a Day whereon mankind will be like moths scattered about,

الْمَنفُوشِ	كَالْعِهْنِ	الْجِبَالُ	وَتَكُونُ
almanfooshi	kaalAAihni	aljibalu	Watakoonu
Carded	Like wool	The mountains	And will be

وَتَكُونُ ٱلْجِبَالُ كَٱلْعِهْنِ ٱلْمَنفُوشِ ٥

5. Watakoonu aljibalu kaalAAihni almanfooshi
And the mountains will be like carded wool,

		مَوَازِينُهُ	ثَقُلَتْ	مَن	فَأَمَّا
		Mawazeenuhu	thaqulat	man	Faamma
		Whose balance	Will be heavy	Him	Then as for

فَأَمَّا مَن ثَقُلَتْ مَوَازِينُهُ ٦

6. Faamma man thaqulat mawazeenuhu
Then as for him whose balance (of good deeds) will be heavy,

		رَّاضِيَةٍ	عِيشَةٍ	فِي	فَهُوَ
		radiyatin	AAeeshatin	fee	Fahuwa
		Pleasant	A life	(will be) in	Then he

فَهُوَ فِي عِيشَةٍ رَّاضِيَةٍ ﴿٧﴾

7. Fahuwa fee AAeeshatin radiyatin
He will live a pleasant life (in Paradise).

		مَوَازِينُهُ	خَفَّتْ	مَنْ	وَأَمَّا
		Mawazeenuhu	khaffat	man	Waamma
		Whose balance	Will be light	Him	But as for

وَأَمَّا مَنْ خَفَّتْ مَوَازِينُهُ ﴿٨﴾

8. Waamma man khaffat mawazeenuhu
But as for him whose balance (of good deeds) will be light,

				هَاوِيَةٌ	فَأُمُّهُ
				hawiyatun	Faommuhu
				(will be) Hell	His abode

فَأُمُّهُ هَاوِيَةٌ ﴿٩﴾

9. Faommuhu hawiyatun
He will have his home in *Hawiyah* (pit, i.e. Hell).

		هِيَهْ	مَا	أَدْرَاكَ	وَمَا
		hiyah	ma	Adraka	Wama
		It is	What	Will make you know	Andwhat

وَمَآ أَدْرَىٰكَ مَا هِيَهْ ﴿١٠﴾

10. Wama adraka ma hiyah
And what will make you know what it is?

				hamiya**tun**	Narun
				حَامِيَةٌ	نَارٌ
				Blazing fiercely	(it is) a fire

نَارٌ حَامِيَةٌ ۝

11. Na̱run hamiya̱tun

(It is) a hot blazing Fire!

Surah # 102
AT-TAKATHUR

Makkia

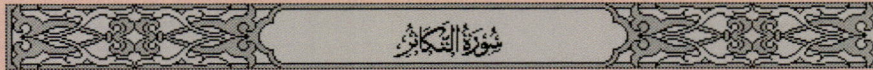

Verses 8
Sections 1

بِسْمِ اللَّهِ الرَّحْمَٰنِ الرَّحِيمِ

				alttaka̱thur**u**	Alha̱kumu
				التَّكَاثُرُ	أَلْهَاكُمُ
				The mutual rivalry (for piling up of worldly things)	Diverts you

أَلْهَٰكُمُ التَّكَاثُرُ ۝

1. Alha̱kumu alttaka̱thuru

The mutual rivalry for piling up of worldly things diverts you,

		almaqa̱bir**a**	zurtumu	Ha̱tta
		الْمَقَابِرَ	زُرْتُمُ	حَتَّىٰ
		The graves	You visit	Until

حَتَّىٰ زُرْتُمُ الْمَقَابِرَ ۝

2. <u>H</u>atta zurtumu almaqabir**a**
Until you visit the graves (i.e. till you die).

			تَعْلَمُونَ	سَوْفَ	كَلَّا
			taAAlamoona	sawfa	Kalla
			You come to know	Shall soon	Nay

كَلَّا سَوْفَ تَعْلَمُونَ ۝

3. Kalla sawfa taAAlamoon**a**
Nay! You shall come to know!

		تَعْلَمُونَ	سَوْفَ	كَلَّا	ثُمَّ
		taAAlamoona	sawfa	kalla	Thumma
		You come to know	Shall soon	Nay	Then

ثُمَّ كَلَّا سَوْفَ تَعْلَمُونَ ۝

4. Thumma kalla sawfa taAAlamoon**a**
Again, Nay! You shall come to know!

الْيَقِينِ	عِلْمَ	تَعْلَمُونَ	لَوْ	كَلَّا
alyaqeen**i**	AAilma	taAAlamoona	law	Kalla
sure	(with) knowledge	You know	If	Nay

كَلَّا لَوْ تَعْلَمُونَ عِلْمَ الْيَقِينِ ۝

5. Kalla law taAAlamoona AAilma alyaqeen**i**
Nay! If you knew with a sure knowledge (the end result of piling up, you would not have occupied yourselves in worldly things)

				الْجَحِيمَ	لَتَرَوُنَّ
				alja<u>h</u>eem**a**	Latarawunna
				The blazing fire (Hell)	Verily you shall see

لَتَرَوُنَّ الْجَحِيمَ ۝

6. Latarawunna alja<u>h</u>eem**a**

Verily, You shall see the blazing Fire (Hell)!

		الْيَقِين	عَيْنَ	لَتَرَوُنَّهَا	ثُمَّ
		alyaqeeni	AAayna	Latarawunnaha	Thumma
		certaintyWith (of) sight		You shall see it	again

$$\text{ثُمَّ لَتَرَوُنَّهَا عَيْنَ ٱلْيَقِينِ ۝}$$

7. Thumma latarawunnaha AAayna alyaqeeni
And again, you shall see it with certainty of sight!

النَّعِيمِ	عَن	يَوْمَئِذٍ	لَتُسْأَلُنَّ	ثُمَّ
alnnaAAeemi	AAani	yawma-ithin	latus-alunna	Thumma
The delight (of the world)	About	On that day	You shall be asked	Then

$$\text{ثُمَّ لَتُسْأَلُنَّ يَوْمَئِذٍ عَنِ ٱلنَّعِيمِ ۝}$$

8. Thumma latus-alunna yawma-ithin AAani alnnaAAeemi
Then, on that Day, you shall be asked about the delight (you indulged in, in this world)!

Surah # 103
AL-ASR
Makkia/Madania

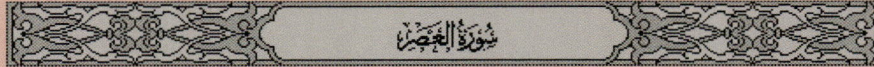

سُورَةُ العَصْر

Verses 3
Sections 1

بِسْمِ اللهِ الرَّحْمٰنِ الرَّحِيمِ

					وَالْعَصْرِ
					WaalAAasri
					By the time

$$\text{وَٱلْعَصْرِ ۝}$$

1. WaalAAasri
By *Al-'Asr* (the time).

		خُسْرٍ	لَفِي	الْإِنسَانَ	إِنَّ
		khusr**in**	lafee	al-ins**a**na	Inna
		Loss	(is) in	Man	Verily

إِنَّ ٱلْإِنسَـٰنَ لَفِي خُسْرٍ ۝

2. Inna al-ins**a**na lafee khusr**in**

Verily! Man is in loss,

وَتَوَاصَوْا	الصَّالِحَاتِ	وَعَمِلُوا	آمَنُوا	الَّذِينَ	إِلَّا
wataw**a**saw	al**s**s**a**lih**a**ti	waAAamiloo	**a**manoo	alla**th**eena	Ill**a**
And recommend one another	Righteous deeds	And do	Believe	Those who	Except

			بِالصَّبْرِ	وَتَوَاصَوْا	بِالْحَقِّ
			bial**s**s**a**bri	wataw**a**saw	bial**h**aqqi
			To patience	And recommend one another	To the truth

إِلَّا ٱلَّذِينَ ءَامَنُوا۟ وَعَمِلُوا۟ ٱلصَّـٰلِحَـٰتِ وَتَوَاصَوْا۟ بِٱلْحَقِّ وَتَوَاصَوْا۟ بِٱلصَّبْرِ ۝

3. Ill**a** alla**th**eena **a**manoo waAAamiloo al**s**s**a**lih**a**ti wataw**a**saw bial**h**aqqi wataw**a**saw bial**s**s**a**bri

Except those who believe (in Islamic Monotheism) and do righteous good deeds, and recommend one another to the truth (i.e. order one another to perform all kinds of good deeds (*Al-Ma'ruf*)which Allah has ordained, and abstain from all kinds of sins and evil deeds (*Al-Munkar*)which Allah has forbidden), and recommend one another to patience (for the sufferings, harms, and injuries which one may encounter in Allah's Cause during preaching His religion of Islamic Monotheism or *Jihad*, etc.).

Surah # 104
AL-HUMAZAH

Makkia

سُورَةُ الْهُمَزَةِ

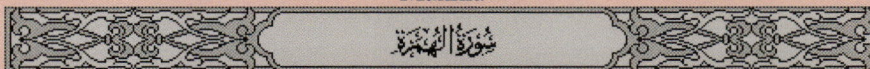

Verses 9
Sections 1

بِسْمِ اللَّهِ الرَّحْمَٰنِ الرَّحِيمِ

		لُمَزَةٍ	هُمَزَةٍ	لِّكُلِّ	وَيْلٌ
		lumaza**tin**	Humaza**tin**	likulli	Waylun
		Backbiter	Slanderer	To every	Woe

وَيْلٌ لِّكُلِّ هُمَزَةٍ لُّمَزَةٍ ﴿١﴾

1. Waylun likulli humaza**tin** lumaza**tin**
Woe to every slanderer and backbiter.

		وَعَدَّدَهُ	مَالًا	جَمَعَ	الَّذِي
		waAAaddada**hu**	m**a**lan	jamaAAa	Alla**thee**
		And counted it	Wealth	Has gathered	Who

الَّذِى جَمَعَ مَالًا وَعَدَّدَهُ ﴿٢﴾

2. Alla**thee** jamaAAa m**a**lan waAAaddadah**u**
Who has gathered wealth and counted it,

		أَخْلَدَهُ	مَالَهُ	أَنَّ	يَحْسَبُ
		akhladah**u**	m**a**lahu	anna	Ya**h**sabu
		Will make him last forever	His wealth	That	He thinks

يَحْسَبُ أَنَّ مَالَهُ أَخْلَدَهُ ﴿٣﴾

3. Ya**h**sabu anna m**a**lahu akhladah**u**
He thinks that his wealth will make him last forever!

		الْحُطَمَةِ	فِي	لَيُنبَذَنَّ	كَلَّا
		al**h**u**t**ama**ti**	fee	layunba**th**anna	Kall**a**
		The crushing fire	Into	Verily he will be thrown	Nay

140

كَلَّا لَيُنۢبَذَنَّ فِى ٱلْحُطَمَةِ ٤

4. Kalla layunbathanna fee alhutamati
Nay! Verily, he will be thrown into the crushing Fire.

		الْحُطَمَةُ	مَا	أَدْرَاكَ	وَمَا
		alhutamatu	ma	adraka	Wama
		The crushing Fire (is)	What	Will make you know	And what

وَمَآ أَدْرَىٰكَ مَا ٱلْحُطَمَةُ ٥

5. Wama adraka ma alhutamatu
And what will make you know what the crushing Fire is?

			الْمُوقَدَةُ	اللّهِ	نَارُ
			almooqadatu	Allahi	Naru
			Kindled	(of) Allah	Fire

نَارُ ٱللَّهِ ٱلْمُوقَدَةُ ٦

6. Naru Allahi almooqadatu
The fire of Allah, kindled,

		الْأَفْئِدَةِ	عَلَى	تَطَّلِعُ	الَّتِى
		al-af-idati	AAala	tattaliAAu	Allatee
		The Hearts	Over	Leaps up	Which

ٱلَّتِى تَطَّلِعُ عَلَى ٱلْأَفْئِدَةِ ٧

7. Allatee tattaliAAu AAala al-af-idati
Which leaps up over the hearts,

		مُّؤْصَدَةٌ	عَلَيْهِم	إِنَّهَا
		mu/sadatun	AAalayhim	Innaha
		Shall be closed	On them	Verily it

141

إِنَّهَا عَلَيْهِم مُّؤْصَدَةٌ ۝

8. Innaha AAalayhim mu/sadatun
Verily, it shall be closed in on them,

			مُّمَدَّدَةٍ	عَمَدٍ	فِي
			mumaddadatin	AAamadin	Fee
			Stretched forth	Pillars	In

فِي عَمَدٍ مُّمَدَّدَةٍ ۝

9. Fee AAamadin mumaddadatin
In pillars stretched forth (i.e. they will be punished in the Fire with pillars, etc.).

Surah # 105
AL-FIL

Makkia

سُورَةُ الفِيل

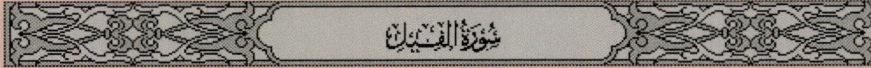

Verses 5
Sections 1

بِسْمِ اللهِ الرَّحْمٰنِ الرَّحِيمِ

بِأَصْحَابِ	رَبُّكَ	فَعَلَ	كَيْفَ	تَرَ	أَلَمْ
bi-as-habi	rabbuka	faAAala	kayfa	tara	Alam
With the owners	Your Lord	Dealt	How	You seen	Have not
					الْفِيلِ
					alfeeli
					(of) the Elephant

أَلَمْ تَرَ كَيْفَ فَعَلَ رَبُّكَ بِأَصْحَابِ ٱلْفِيلِ ۝

142

1. Alam tara kayfa faAAala rabbuka bi-as-habi alfeeli

Have you (O Muhammad (ﷺ)) not seen how your Lord dealt with the Owners of the Elephant? [The elephant army which came from Yemen under the command of Abrahah Al-Ashram intending to destroy the Ka'bah at Makkah].

أَلَمْ	يَجْعَلْ	كَيْدَهُمْ	فِي	تَضْلِيلٍ
Alam	yajAAal	kaydahum	fee	tadleelin
Did not	He make	Their plot	(in)	Go astray

أَلَمْ يَجْعَلْ كَيْدَهُمْ فِي تَضْلِيلٍ ﴿٢﴾

2. Alam yajAAal kaydahum fee tadleelin
Did He not make their plot go astray?

ع وَأَرْسَلَ	عَلَيْهِمْ	طَيْرًا	أَبَابِيلَ
Waarsala	AAalayhim	tayran	ababeela
And He sent	Against them	Birds	In flocks

وَأَرْسَلَ عَلَيْهِمْ طَيْرًا أَبَابِيلَ ﴿٣﴾

3. Waarsala AAalayhim tayran ababeela
And sent against them birds, in flocks,

تَرْمِيهِم	بِحِجَارَةٍ	مِّن	سِجِّيلٍ
Tarmeehim	bihijaratin	min	Sijjeelin
Striking them	With stones	Of	Baked clay

تَرْمِيهِم بِحِجَارَةٍ مِّن سِجِّيلٍ ﴿٤﴾

4. Tarmeehim bihijaratin min sijjeelin
Striking them with stones of *Sijjil*.

فَجَعَلَهُمْ	كَعَصْفٍ	مَّأْكُولٍ
FajaAAalahum	kaAAasfin	ma/koolin
And made them	Like stubble , stalks	(eaten up) devoured

فَجَعَلَهُمْ كَعَصْفٍ مَّأْكُولٍ ﴿٥﴾

5. FajaAAalahum kaAAasfin ma/koolin

And made them like an empty field of stalks (of which the corn has been eaten up by cattle).

Surah # 106
QURAISH

Makkia

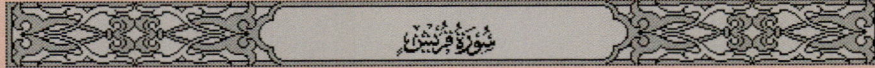

سُورَةُ قُرَيْش

Verses 4
Sections 1

بِسْمِ اللهِ الرَّحْمٰنِ الرَّحِيمِ

				قُرَيْشٍ	لِإِيلَافِ
				qurayshin	Li-eelafi
				(of) Quraish	for the safety

لِإِيلَفِ قُرَيْشٍ ۝

1. Li-eelafi qurayshin

(It is a great Grace (from Allah), for the protection of the Quraish,

		وَالصَّيْفِ	الشِّتَاءِ	رِحْلَةَ	إِيلَافِهِمْ
		waalssayfi	alshshita-i	Rihlata	Eelafihim
		And summer	(of) winter	The journeying	(for) their safety

إِۦلَفِهِمْ رِحْلَةَ ٱلشِّتَآءِ وَٱلصَّيْفِ ۝

2. Eelafihim rihlata alshshita-i waalssayfi

(And with all those Allah's Grace and Protections for their traveling, We cause) the (Quraish) caravans to set forth safe in winter (to the south), and in summer (to the north without any fear),

		الْبَيْتِ	هَذَا	رَبَّ	فَلْيَعْبُدُوا
		Albayti	hatha	rabba	FalyaAAudoo
		House (the	(of) this	The Lord	So let them

		Kabah)			worship

فَلْيَعْبُدُواْ رَبَّ هَـٰذَا ٱلْبَيْتِ ﴿٣﴾

3. FalyaAAbudoo rabba hatha albayti
So let them worship (Allah) the Lord of this House (the Ka'bah in Makkah).

مِّنْ	وَآمَنَهُم	جُوعٍ	مِّن	أَطْعَمَهُم	الَّذِي
min	waamanahum	jooAAin	min	atAAamahum	Allathee
From	And has made them safe	Hunger	Against	Has fed them	(He) who

					خَوْفٍ
					khawfin
					Fear

ٱلَّذِىٓ أَطْعَمَهُم مِّن جُوعٍ وَءَامَنَهُم مِّنْ خَوْفٍ ﴿٤﴾

4. Allathee atAAamahum min jooAAin waamanahum min khawfin
(He) Who has fed them against hunger, and has made them safe from fear.

Surah # 107
AL-MA'UN

Makkia/Madania

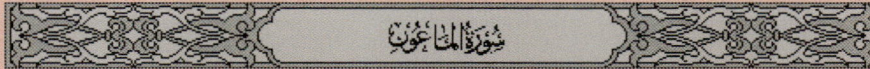

سُورَةُ الْمَاعُونِ

بِسْمِ اللهِ الرَّحْمَنِ الرَّحِيمِ

		بِالدِّينِ	يُكَذِّبُ	الَّذِي	أَرَأَيْتَ
		bialddeeni	yukaththibu	allathee	Araayta
		The Recompense	Denies	Him who	Have you seen

أَرَءَيْتَ ٱلَّذِى يُكَذِّبُ بِٱلدِّينِ ﴿١﴾

1. Araayta allathee yukaththibu bialddeeni
Have you seen him who denies the Recompense?

145

		الْيَتِيمَ	يَدُعُّ	الَّذِي	فَذَلِكَ
		Alyateema	yaduAAAAu	allathee	Fathalika
		The orphan	Repulses	(he) who	That is

فَذَلِكَ ٱلَّذِى يَدُعُّ ٱلْيَتِيمَ ۝

2. Fathalika allathee yaduAAAAu alyateema
That is he who repulses the orphan (harshly),

الْمِسْكِينِ	طَعَامِ	عَلَى	يَحُضُّ	وَلَا
almiskeeni	taAAami	AAala	yahuddu	Wala
(of) the poor	Feeding	On	Urges	And not

وَلَا تَحُضُّ عَلَى طَعَامِ ٱلْمِسْكِينِ ۝

3. Wala yahuddu AAala taAAami almiskeeni
And urges not the feeding of *AlMiskin* (the poor),

			لِّلْمُصَلِّينَ	فَوَيْلٌ
			lilmusalleena	Fawaylun
			Unto those performers of prayers	So woe

فَوَيْلٌ لِّلْمُصَلِّينَ ۝

4. Fawaylun lilmusalleena
So woe unto those performers of *Salat* (prayers) (hypocrites),

سَاهُونَ	صَلَاتِهِمْ	عَن	هُمْ	الَّذِينَ
sahoona	salatihim	AAan	Hum	Allatheena
(are) heedless	Their prayer	Of	(they)	Those who

ٱلَّذِينَ هُمْ عَن صَلَاتِهِمْ سَاهُونَ ۝

5. Allatheena hum AAan salatihim sahoona
Who delay their *Salat* (prayer) from their stated fixed times,

		يُرَاؤُونَ	هُمْ	الَّذِينَ

			yuraoona	hum	Allatheena
			(do good deeds) to be seen	(they)	Those who

ٱلَّذِينَ هُمْ يُرَآؤُونَ ۝

6. Allatheena hum yuraoona

Those who do good deeds only to be seen (of men),

				الْمَاعُونَ	وَيَمْنَعُونَ
				almaAAoona	WayamnaAAoona
				Small kindness (untensils)	And they withhold

وَيَمْنَعُونَ ٱلْمَاعُونَ ۝

7. WayamnaAAoona almaAAoona

And refuse *Al-Ma'un* (small kindnesses e.g. salt, sugar, water, etc.).

Surah # 108
AL-KAUTHAR

Makkia

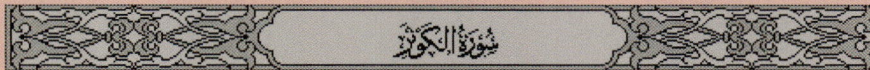

سُورَةُ الْكَوْثَرِ

Verses 3
Sections 1

بِسْمِ اللهِ الرَّحْمٰنِ الرَّحِيمِ

			الْكَوْثَرَ	أَعْطَيْنَاكَ	إِنَّا
			alkawthara	aAAtaynaka	Inna
			Al-kauthar (a river in paradise)	Have granted you	Verily we

إِنَّا أَعْطَيْنَاكَ ٱلْكَوْثَرَ ۝

1. Inna aAAtaynaka alkawthara

Verily, We have granted you (O Muhammad (ﷺ)) *Al-Kauthar* (a river in Paradise);

			وَٱنْحَرْ	لِرَبِّكَ	فَصَلِّ
			wainhar	lirabbika	Fasalli
			And sacrifice	To your Lord	Therefore turn in prayer

فَصَلِّ لِرَبِّكَ وَٱنْحَرْ ۝

2. Fasalli lirabbika wainhar

Therefore turn in prayer to your Lord and sacrifice (to Him only).

		ٱلْأَبْتَرُ	هُوَ	شَانِئَكَ	إِنَّ
		al-abtaru	Huwa	shani-aka	Inna
		Cut off/ childless	(he)	Your traducer	For/ verily

إِنَّ شَانِئَكَ هُوَ ٱلْأَبْتَرُ ۝

3. Inna shani-aka huwa al-abtaru

For he who makes you angry (O Muhammad (ﷺ)), - he will be cut off (from every good thing in this world and in the Hereafter).

Surah # 109
AL-KAFIRUN
Makkia

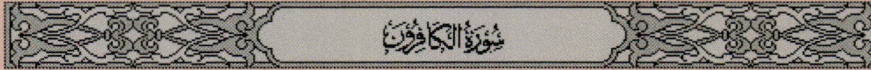

Verses 6

Sections 1

بِسْمِ اللهِ الرَّحْمٰنِ الرَّحِيمِ

		الْكَافِرُونَ	أَيُّهَا	يَا	قُلْ
		alkafiroona	ayyuha	ya	Qul
		Disbelievers	you	O!	Say

قُلْ يَا أَيُّهَا الْكَافِرُونَ ۝

1. Qul ya ayyuha alkafiroona

Say (O Muhammad ﷺ) to these *Mushrikun* and *Kafirun*): "O *Al-Kafirun* (disbelievers in Allah, in His Oneness, in His Angels, in His Books, in His Messengers, in the Day of Resurrection, and in *Al-Qadar*, etc.)!

		تَعْبُدُونَ	مَا	أَعْبُدُ	لَا
		taAAbudoona	ma	aAAbudu	La
		You worship	That which	I shall worship	Not

لَا أَعْبُدُ مَا تَعْبُدُونَ ۝

2. La aAAbudu ma taAAbudoona

"I worship not that which you worship,

	أَعْبُدُ	مَا	عَابِدُونَ	أَنتُمْ	وَلَا
	aAAbudu	Ma	AAabidoona	antum	Wala
	I worship	That which	Will worship	You	Nor

وَلَا أَنتُمْ عَابِدُونَ مَا أَعْبُدُ ۝

3. Wala antum AAabidoona ma aAAbudu

"Nor will you worship that which I worship.

أَعْبُدُ	عَبَدتُّمْ	مَّا	عَابِدٌ	أَنَا	وَلَا
	AAabadtum	ma	AAabidun	ana	Wala
	You are worshiping	That which	Shall worship	I	And not

وَلَا أَنَا عَابِدٌ مَّا عَبَدتُّمْ ۝

4. Wala ana AAabidun ma AAabadtum

"And I shall not worship that which you are worshipping.

أَعْبُدُ	مَا	عَابِدُونَ	أَنتُمْ	وَلَا
aAAbud**u**	m**a**	AA**a**bidoona	antum	Wal**a**
I worship	That which	Will worship	You	Nor

وَلَا أَنتُمْ عَابِدُونَ مَآ أَعْبُدُ ۝

5. Wal**a** antum AA**a**bidoona m**a** aAAbud**u**

"Nor will you worship that which I worship.

		دِينِ	وَلِيَ	دِينُكُمْ	لَكُمْ
		deen**i**	waliya	deenukum	Lakum
		My religion	And to me	(be) your religion	To you

لَكُمْ دِينُكُمْ وَلِيَ دِينِ ۝

6. Lakum deenukum waliya deen**i**

"To you be your religion, and to me my religion (Islamic Monotheism)."

Surah # 110
AN-NASR

Madania

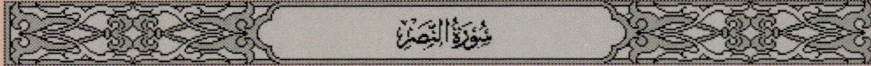

سُورَةُ النَّصْر

Verses 3
Sections 1

بِسْمِ اللهِ الرَّحْمَٰنِ الرَّحِيمِ

وَالْفَتْحُ	اللهِ	نَصْرُ	جَاءَ	إِذَا
waalfath**u**	All**a**hi	na**s**ru	j**aa**	Ith**a**
And the triumph/victory	(of) Allah	The Help	Comes	When

إِذَا جَاءَ نَصْرُ ٱللَّهِ وَٱلْفَتْحُ ۝

1. Ith**a** j**aa** na**s**ru All**a**hi waalfath**u**

When comes the Help of Allah (to you, O Muhammad (ﷺ) against your enemies) and the conquest (of Makkah),

اللَّهِ	دِينِ	فِي	يَدْخُلُونَ	النَّاسَ	وَرَأَيْتَ
Allahi	deeni	fee	yadkhuloona	alnnasa	Waraayta
(of) Allah	Religion	In	Entering	The people	And you see
				أَفْوَاجًا	
				afwajan	
				In crowds	

وَرَأَيْتَ ٱلنَّاسَ يَدْخُلُونَ فِي دِينِ ٱللَّهِ أَفْوَاجًا ﴿٢﴾

2. Waraayta alnnasa yadkhuloona fee deeni Allahi afwajan

And you see that the people enter Allah's religion (Islam) in crowds,

كَانَ	إِنَّهُ	وَاسْتَغْفِرْهُ	رَبِّكَ	بِحَمْدِ	فَسَبِّحْ
kana	innahu	waistaghfirhu	rabbika	bihamdi	Fasabbih
Is	Verily He	And ask His Forgiveness	(of) your Lord	The praises	So glorify
					تَوَّابًا
					tawwaban
					Oft-Forgiving

فَسَبِّحْ بِحَمْدِ رَبِّكَ وَٱسْتَغْفِرْهُ إِنَّهُ كَانَ تَوَّابًا ﴿٣﴾

3. Fasabbih bihamdi rabbika waistaghfirhu innahu kana tawwaban

So glorify the Praises of your Lord, and ask for His Forgiveness. Verily, He is the One Who accepts the repentance and forgives.

Surah # 111
AL-MASAD

Makkia

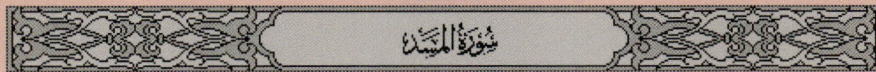

سُورَةُ المَسَدِ

Verses 5

Section 1

بِسْمِ اللَّهِ الرَّحْمَٰنِ الرَّحِيمِ

تَبَّتْ	يَدَا	أَبِي	لَهَبٍ	وَتَبَّ

	watabba	lahabin	abee	yada	Tabbat
	And perish he	Lahab	(of) Abu	The two hands	Perish

بِسْمِ﴿ تَبَّتۡ يَدَآ أَبِى لَهَبٖ وَتَبَّ ١﴾

1. Tabbat yada abee lahabin watabba
Perish the two hands of Abu Lahab (an uncle of the Prophet), and perish he!

كَسَبَ	وَمَا	مَالُهُ	عَنۡهُ	أَغۡنَىٰ	مَا
kasaba	Wama	maluhu	AAanhu	aghna	Ma
He earned	And what	His wealth	Him	Will benefit	Not

مَآ أَغۡنَىٰ عَنۡهُ مَالُهُۥ وَمَا كَسَبَ ٢

2. Ma aghna AAanhu maluhu wama kasaba
His wealth and his children (etc.) will not benefit him!

		لَهَب	ذَاتَ	نَارًا	سَيَصۡلَىٰ
		lahabin	thata	naran	Sayasla
		Blazing flames	Of	In a fire	He will be burnt

سَيَصۡلَىٰ نَارٗا ذَاتَ لَهَبٖ ٣

3. Sayasla naran thata lahabin
He will be burnt in a Fire of blazing flames!

		الۡحَطَب	حَمَّالَةَ	وَامۡرَأَتُهُ
		alhatabi	hammalata	Waimraatuhu
		(of) wood	(who is) carrier	And his wife

وَامۡرَأَتُهُۥ حَمَّالَةَ ٱلۡحَطَبِ ٤

4. Waimraatuhu hammalata alhatabi
And his wife too, who carries wood (thorns of *Sadan* which she used to put on the way of the Prophet (ﷺ), or use to slander him).

مَّسَدِ	مِّن	حَبۡلٌ	جِيدِهَا	فِي

	masadin	min	hablun	jeediha	Fee
	Palm fibre	Of	(will be) twisted rope	Her neck	In

فِى جِيدِهَا حَبْلٌ مِّن مَّسَدٍ ۝

5. Fee jeediha hablun min masadin

In her neck is a twisted rope of *Masad* (palm fibre).

Surah # 112
AL-IKHLAS
Makkia

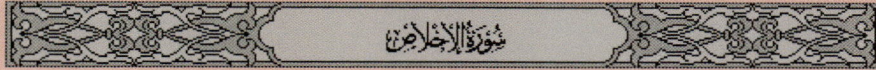

Verses 4

Sections 1

بِسْمِ اللهِ الرَّحْمَنِ الرَّحِيمِ

		ahadun	Allahu	huwa	Qul
		That one	(is) Allah	He	Say

قُلْ هُوَ اللَّهُ أَحَدٌ ۝

1. Qul huwa Allahu ahadun

Say (O Muhammad (ﷺ)): "He is Allah, (the) One.

				alssamadu	Allahu
				The self-sufficient	Allah

اللَّهُ الصَّمَدُ ۝

2. Allahu alssamadu

"*Allah-us-Samad* (The Self-Sufficient Master, Whom all creatures need, He neither eats nor drinks).

153

		يُولَدْ	وَلَمْ	يَلِدْ	لَمْ
		yooladu	walam	Yalid	Lam
		He was begotten	Nor	He begets	Not

$$\text{لَمْ يَلِدْ وَلَمْ يُولَدْ } ۝$$

3. Lam yalid walam yooladu

"He begets not, nor was He begotten;

أَحَدٌ	كُفُوًا	لَّهُ	يَكُن	وَلَمْ
ahadun	kufuwan	lahu	yakun	Walam
Anyone	Co-equal or comparable	Unto Him	And there is not	

$$\text{وَلَمْ يَكُن لَّهُ كُفُوًا أَحَدٌ } ۝$$

4. Walam yakun lahu kufuwan ahadun

"And there is none co-equal or comparable unto Him."

Surah # 113
AL-FALAQ

Makkia/Madania

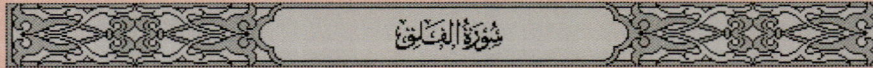

سُورَةُ الفَلَقِ

Verses 5

Sections 1

بِسْمِ اللّٰهِ الرَّحْمٰنِ الرَّحِيمِ

		الْفَلَقِ	بِرَبِّ	أَعُوذُ	قُلْ
		alfalaqi	birabbi	aAAoothu	Qul
		(of) the day-break	With the Lord	I seek refuge	Say

$$\text{قُلْ أَعُوذُ بِرَبِّ الْفَلَقِ } ۝$$

1. Qul aAAoothu birabbi alfalaqi

Say: "I seek refuge with (Allah) the Lord of the daybreak,

		خَلَقَ	مَا	شَرٌّ	مِن
		khalaqa	ma	sharri	Min
		He has created	(of) what	The evil	From

مِن شَرِّ مَا خَلَقَ ﴿٢﴾

2. Min sharri ma khalaqa

"From the evil of what He has created;

وَقَبَ	إِذَا	غَاسِقٍ	شَرٌّ	وَمِن
waqaba	Itha	ghasiqin	sharri	Wamin
It is intense	As/when	(of) darkness	The evil	And from

وَمِن شَرِّ غَاسِقٍ إِذَا وَقَبَ ﴿٣﴾

3. Wamin sharri ghasiqin itha waqaba

"And from the evil of the darkening (night) as it comes with its darkness; (or the moon as it sets or goes away).

الْعُقَدِ	فِي	النَّفَّاثَاتِ	شَرٌّ	وَمِن
alAAuqadi	fee	alnnaffathati	sharri	Wamin
The knots	In	(of) the witches who blow	The evil	And from

وَمِن شَرِّ ٱلنَّفَّٰثَٰتِ فِي ٱلْعُقَدِ ﴿٤﴾

4. Wamin sharri alnnaffathati fee alAAuqadi

"And from the evil of the witchcrafts when they blow in the knots,

حَسَدَ	إِذَا	حَاسِدٍ	شَرٌّ	وَمِن
Hasada	itha	hasidin	sharri	Wamin
He envies	When	(of) envier	The evil	And from

وَمِن شَرِّ حَاسِدٍ إِذَا حَسَدَ ﴿٥﴾

5. Wamin sharri hasidin itha hasada

"And from the evil of the envier when he envies."

Surah # 114
AN-NAS

Makkia/Madania

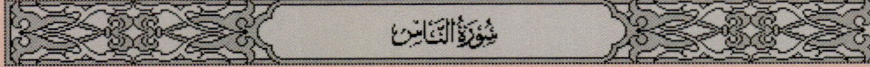

سُورَةُ النَّاسِ

Verses 6
Sections 1

بِسْمِ اللَّهِ الرَّحْمَٰنِ الرَّحِيمِ

		النَّاسِ	بِرَبِّ	أَعُوذُ	قُلْ
		alnnasi	birabbi	aAAoothu	Qul
		(of) mankind	With the Lord	I seek refuge	Say

قُلْ أَعُوذُ بِرَبِّ ٱلنَّاسِ ﴿١﴾

1. Qul aAAoothu birabbi alnnasi
Say: "I seek refuge with (Allah) the Lord of mankind,

				النَّاسِ	مَلِكِ
				alnnasi	Maliki
				(of) mankind	The king

مَلِكِ ٱلنَّاسِ ﴿٢﴾

2. Maliki alnnasi
"The King of mankind,

				النَّاسِ	إِلَٰهِ
				alnnasi	Ilahi
				(of) Mankind	The Ilah (God)

إِلَٰهِ ٱلنَّاسِ ﴿٣﴾

3. Ilahi alnnasi
"The *Ilah* (God) of mankind,

الْخَنَّاسِ	الْوَسْوَاسِ	شَرِّ	مِن
	alkhannasi	alwaswasi	sharri	Min
	Sneaking	(of) the whisperer	The evil	From

مِن شَرِّ ٱلْوَسْوَاسِ ٱلْخَنَّاسِ ۝

4. Min sharri alwaswasi alkhannasi

"From the evil of the whisperer (devil who whispers evil in the hearts of men) who withdraws (from his whispering in one's heart after one remembers Allah) ,

النَّاسِ	صُدُورِ	فِي	يُوَسْوِسُ	الَّذِي
	alnnasi	Sudoori	fee	yuwaswisu	Allathee
	(of) mankind	The breasts	In	Whispers	Who

ٱلَّذِى يُوَسْوِسُ فِى صُدُورِ ٱلنَّاسِ ۝

5. Allathee yuwaswisu fee sudoori alnnasi

"Who whispers in the breasts of mankind,

النَّاسِ	وَ	الْجِنَّةِ	مِنَ
		waalnnasi	aljinnati	Mina
		And men	Jinn	Of /from

مِنَ ٱلْجِنَّةِ وَٱلنَّاسِ ۝

6. Mina aljinnati waalnnasi

"Of jinns and men."

Dua at the Completion of Qur'an

O! Allah! In my grave change my fear into love. O! Allah! Have mercy on me in the name of this great Qur'an: and make it for me a Guide, a Light, and a Source of your Guisance and Mercy: O! Allah! Make me remember what of it I have forgotten, make me know of it that which I have become ignorant of: and make me recite it in the hours of night and the day: and make it an argument in my favor. O! Sustainer of all the worlds.

A'meen

Talib-e-Dua
Dr. Syed Viquaruddin Hasan
svhusa@gmail.com

Printed in Great Britain
by Amazon

45462901R00091